JUNIOR CERTIFIC

English Revision

Ordinary Level

Louise O'Reilly

Gill & Macmillan

Gill & Macmillan
Hume Avenue
Park West
Dublin 12
with associated companies throughout the world
www.gillmacmillan.ie

978 07171 4679 6

Design by Liz White Designs
Print origination by O'K Graphic Design, Dublin

The paper used in this book is made from the wood pulp of managed forests. For every tree felled, at least one tree is planted, thereby renewing natural resources.

For permission to reproduce photographs, the author and publisher gratefully acknowledge the following:

© Advertising Archives: 90L; © Alamy: 6, 76T, 76B, 77; © The Bridgeman Art Library: 15; © Corbis: 37, 38T, 38B, 66; © Getty Images: 1, 3, 58, 60, 61, 63, 65, 71, 100CL, 100T, 100CR, 100B; © Irish Times: 102B; © Munch Museum/Munch - Ellingsen Group, BONO, Oslo/DACS, London 2011: 15; © Press Association: 97BL; © Photolibrary: 17; © Reuters: 97TR, 97BR; Courtesy of Coca Cola: 90C; Courtesy of Apple: 90R; Courtesy of Heat Magazine: 103; Courtesy of the Evening Herald: 102T; Courtesy of the State Examination Commission: 92T, 92B, 93T, 93B, 97TL, 97CL, 97BC, 97C, 97CR.

The authors and publisher have made every effort to trace all copyright holders, but if any has been inadvertently overlooked we would be pleased to make the necessary arrangement at the first opportunity.

CONTENTS

Introduction

A guide to the exam structure

The Junior Certificate English Ordinary Level exam is a two-and-a-half-hour exam divided into seven sections. You have approximately 25 minutes per section.

Sections 1, 2, 3 and 4 **must** be answered. Section 1 is always Reading, Section 2 is always Personal Writing and Section 3 is always Functional Writing. Section 4 changes each year but whatever topic comes up in Section 4 (Poetry or Drama or Fiction or Media Studies), you must answer this section. Sections 5, 6 and 7 vary in topic, but you have to answer just two of these three sections. So in Sections 5, 6 and 7, you can leave out one section.

Exam timetable

Allow yourself 25 minutes per section. If you have any spare time at the end of the exam, you should use it to check through your work.

Your timetable for the exam breaks down like this:

9.30	Section 1*	Reading
9.55	Section 2*	Personal Writing (essay)
10.20	Section 3*	Functional Writing
10.45	Section 4* }	Poetry **or**
11.10	Section 5 }	Drama **or**
11.35	Section 6 }	Fiction **or**
	Section 7 }	Media Studies
12.00	Finish	

* Sections 1-4 must be answered. Choose **two** out of the remaining three sections to answer.

Poetry, Drama, Fiction or Media Studies may appear in Section 4 of the paper. Whichever one appears in Section 4 must be answered.

It is very important that you stick to allowing yourself only 25 minutes for each section. Each section carries 60 marks and you will be doing yourself no favours by spending an hour finishing off that thrilling four-page essay and leaving out all of a later section! It is up to you to move on to the next section as soon as your 25 minutes are up. Some sections may take you less than 25 minutes and you can use that extra time to go back at the end and finish any sections you didn't fully finish.

Don't waste time answering every section. Decide at the beginning which section (5 or 6 or 7) you are going to leave out. You won't get any extra marks for answering every section.

Key words

There are certain words that are always used in the exam questions. The following examples are used regularly, so make sure you understand exactly what is being asked in each case:

- **Composition:** This means your essay or story. This is used in the Personal Writing section, e.g. 'Write a *composition* on one of the following topics...'
- **Convey:** This means to show or express, e.g. 'How does the poet *convey* sadness in the poem?' In this case you are really being asked how the poet shows that he/she is sad in the poem.
- **Dialogue:** This means to write out the conversation like a script, e.g.
  Joe: Hi Mary!
  Mary: Hi Joe, how are you?
- **Image/Imagery:** This relates to the pictures formed in your head from reading the poem, story, etc. This does not mean the pictures on the exam paper. The question 'Choose an image that you like from the poem' is asking you to choose a line from the poem that creates a picture in your head that you like.
- **Reference:** You may be asked to support your answer with reference to the text. This means that you can use the words or lines from the poem or story to prove your point.
- **Stanza:** This means the verse of a poem.

There are other key words in each section that regularly appear in the exam. These will be highlighted at the end of each chapter.

1 Reading

- To be able to approach the Reading section with confidence.
- To know exactly what the examiner is looking for in your answers.

In this section you will be given a **short extract** to read and will be asked to answer the **five questions** that follow. As this is the first section of the first exam that you will sit in your Junior Certificate, it is designed to be as straightforward as possible. There is no reason why you shouldn't gain full marks on this section as long as you follow a few basic guidelines:

- **Read the extract carefully**. Make sure you understand exactly what the extract is about. If there are any words you don't understand, read the entire sentence again – you may be able to work out the meaning of the word from the sentence.
- **Read the question carefully**. You cannot gain marks if you don't answer exactly what is being asked. If you are asked to give reasons for your answer, then you will need to give at least two reasons.
- **Use full sentences in your answer.** At Ordinary Level you are expected to write in full sentences – you may lose some marks for not doing so.
- **Use the marks given as a guideline.** If a question is worth only 5 marks, then you need to write only a sentence or two. If it is worth 10 marks, you need to write a paragraph or 5–10 lines, and a 20–mark question requires at least two paragraphs or 10–20 lines.
- **Be neat.** Don't have your answers all crowded together – use the space in your answer book to separate them out. You should try to create a good first impression. Keep your writing neat and easy to read. Stay between the margins. The answer book has margins on both sides of the page. The margins on the right-hand side are for the examiners, so leave them blank.
- **Be aware of spelling and punctuation.** If there are words that you often spell incorrectly, then learn how to spell them correctly now. Have a look at the last chapter of this book to see the most common mistakes made by students – and try to avoid making them yourself!

The questions

Question A is usually broken down into **four short questions**, each worth 5 marks. The questions usually refer to factual information in the extract. Your answers should be **full sentences**. Try to put the information in your own words if possible, rather than just writing out the sentence from the passage.

Most students should score full marks on this question.

The other four questions will assess your understanding of the text. You will be asked to find certain information in the passage and may be asked to give your opinion on some aspects of the piece.

Find information

In this type of question you will be asked to find out certain facts from the extract and you will usually be told what paragraph of the text to look in. **Take your answer only from the paragraph mentioned.** Also, try to put the information in your own words rather than just copying down the entire paragraph.

Explain the phrases

In this type of question you will usually be given four phrases or sentences, and will be asked to explain two. Each explanation is worth 5 marks. In your answers, make sure you use other words, rather than reusing the words given. If you are not sure what the phrase means, read the paragraph it comes from, as this may give you a better idea of the meaning of the phrase.

What is the main idea of the extract?

In this type of question you may be asked to pick a topic from a list of three and explain why you think this is the main idea of the passage. Make sure you can give at least two reasons why you think whichever one you choose is correct. Don't be afraid to quote from the extract to support your reasons.

Give your opinion

You may be asked to give your opinion on various aspects of the passage. For example, you may be asked what type of person you think the writer is. You may also be asked to discuss a topic or to give your opinion on the topic in the passage. Make sure you give reasons from the passage to support your own opinion.

Sample exam questions and answers

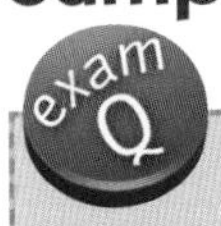

Read the following extract, taken from the 2009 exam paper, and examine the questions that follow.

Fifty Years of Tidy Towns

1. The first Tidy Towns Competition was held in Ireland in 1958. The focus right from the start was to encourage communities to improve their local environment and make their area a better place to live and work in, and to visit.

2. The first competition attracted entries from 52 towns and villages, and was won by the County Donegal town of Glenties. In fact Glenties went on to win the top prize again in 1959, 1960, 1962 and 1995. Over the years the competition has rapidly increased in popularity with an average of 700 entrants each year.

3. So many people participate in preparing the local area for the adjudication that it is impossible to accurately estimate the number of people who have been involved, but it is safe to say that in over 50 years it has run into hundreds of thousands.

4. The Tidy Towns Competition is open to all areas: big or small, urban or rural. Places are entered in different categories depending on the size of their population. Categories range from the smallest, Category A, which caters for places with fewer than 200 residents, up to the largest, Category H, which is for areas with more than 25,000 people.

5. Judging takes place during June, July and August each year. The prize fund now runs to some €250,000. Prizes are awarded in many different categories including best new entrant, county awards, gold, silver and bronze medals.

6. There are separate award sections for island and Gaeltacht entrants. The top prize and title of 'Ireland's Tidiest Town' goes to the highest scoring entrant in the whole competition.

7. Praising the competition, Minister for the Environment John Gormley, TD, has said that the original founders were 'visionaries' and that the competition has made Ireland not just a cleaner country, but a more civic-minded and confident place.

Source: Adapted from Kieran Fagan, *The Irish Times, Special Report,* 18 September 2008

Sample questions

A. 1. Why was the Tidy Towns Competition set up? (5)
   2. Which town won the first competition? (5)
   3. How many entrants are there on average each year? (5)
   4. When does the judging take place? (5)

Factual information questions

B. From your reading of the passage give two reasons why the Tidy Towns Competition has been successful. (10)

C. Explain any **TWO** of the following in your own words:
   1. The focus right from the start was to encourage communities to improve their local environment. (paragraph 1)
   2. The prize fund now runs to some €250,000. (paragraph 5)
   3. ... the competition has rapidly increased in popularity (paragraph 2)
   4. ... preparing the local area for the adjudication (paragraph 3) (10)

D. What do you think Minister for the Environment John Gormley, TD, meant when he said that the original founders were 'visionaries'? (10)

E. 'The Tidy Towns Competition has made Ireland a better place.'
   Write a paragraph either for **OR** against this point of view. (10)

Opinion question

exam focus

Answering opinion questions:

If you are asked to give your opinion on the passage, use sentences lik the following to frame your answer:

I agree with the writer when he/she said...

I think that the writer wa correct when he/she said..

I disagree with the writer as I feel that...

In my opinion, ...

Sample answers

A. 1. ***Why** was the Tidy Towns Competition set up?* (5)
   The Tidy Towns Competition was set up **to get communities to look after and improve their local area.** This would help to make their area a better place to live and work in and to visit.
   2. ***Which** town won the first competition?* (5)
   The first town to win the competition was **Glenties** in County Donegal.
   3. ***How many** entrants are there on average each year?* (5)
   There are an average of **700** entrants each year.
   4. ***When** does judging take place?* (5)
   The judging takes place in **June, July and August** each year.

key point

Find the factua information in the passage anc use full sentences.

B. *From your reading of the passage give **two reasons** why the Tidy Towns Competition has been successful.* (10)

From my reading of the passage, I think the Tidy Towns Competition has been so successful because **firstly**, the focus has been on communities improving their local environment, making their area a better place to live and work in and to visit. **Secondly**, the Tidy Towns Competition has been successful as it is open to all areas big or small, urban or rural, and prizes are awarded in many different categories.

C. *Explain any **TWO** of the following in your own words:*

1. *The focus right from the start was to encourage communities to improve their local environment. (paragraph 1)*
2. *The prize fund now runs to some €250,000. (paragraph 5)*
3. *...the competition has rapidly increased in popularity (paragraph 2)*
4. *...preparing the local area for the adjudication (paragraph 3)* (10)

1. This means that from the very beginning the aim of the competition was to get communitites to make their local areas better.
2. This means that the amount of money given in prizes is more than 250,000 euro.

D. *What do you think Minister for the Environment John Gormley, TD, meant when he said that the original founders were 'visionaries'?* (10)

I think John Gormley meant that the original founders were thinking of the future and that they acted in a way that made the country a better place in which to live. To be 'visionaries' means that they had a clear vision of what they thought the future should be like.

E. *'The Tidy Towns Competition has made Ireland a better place.' Write a paragraph either for **OR** against this point of view.* (10)

I agree with this point of view. I think the Tidy Towns Competition has made Ireland a better place. Thousands of people get involved in the competition in their local areas. The work that they do cleaning up public places, planting flowers and improving their local areas makes a big difference. There are over 700 entrants each year and the competition is open to all areas, big or small. This means that most areas throughout the country are involved in the competition. For these reasons, I think that the Tidy Towns Competition has made Ireland a better place.

Use the information in the passage to support your answer, e.g. There are over 700 entrants.

Practice questions

Read the following extracts and attempt the questions that follow.
Before you begin, remember to:

- Read the passage carefully.
- Read the questions and underline the key words.
- Reread the passage and underline the words, phrases or sections that may be useful in your answers.
- Be neat with your answers.
- Use full sentences.
- Only allow yourself 25 minutes to complete the section.

Practice question 1

Pirates (Junior Certificate Ordinary Level 2008)

Pirates are the robbers of the sea. They have flourished for thousands of years wherever rich, defenceless ships have sailed. Pirates have always been eager to get their hands on anything of value from gold bars and coins to spices and silks and, nowadays, arms and electronic equipment. The most famous pirate stories are about rough villains swigging rum beneath their black flag with its skull and crossbones, while their terrified captives are forced to walk the plank, and parrots squawk of buried treasure and revenge.

The ideal pirate hunting ground is to be found where there is a busy, narrow shipping channel, plenty of hidden coves for unloading booty, and waters that are not very well patrolled. The best-known haunts for pirates were the Indian Ocean, the seas of the Far East and, most famous of all, the Caribbean.

Pirates make wonderful subjects for films. Film makers are usually more concerned with a good story than with telling the truth and the pirates that they show have perfect, gleaming white teeth and well-groomed hair; they are always ready to rescue beautiful women and act like gentlemen – a far cry from reality!

The world of the pirate has almost always been exclusively male. However, there have been some remarkable exceptions such as Grace O'Malley, the 'Pirate Queen' from County Galway who attacked English ships for a period of over twenty-five years during the sixteenth century.

Piracy still exists even though modern means of patrol have made piracy a much more risky business than it was in the past. However, the pirates of today use very high-tech equipment, and attacks by them on merchant ships off the coasts of Brazil, West Africa, the islands of Southeast Asia and the Caribbean are still alarmingly common. The smaller the vessel, the more likely it is to be attacked. Speed is the principal tactic. Pirates roar out from concealed inlets in high-speed power boats and threaten their victims with guns and rockets.

So it seems that as long as there are ships carrying valuable cargo, there will be pirates.

Source: *Pirates – Fact or Fiction* by Stewart Ross

Questions

A. Find answers to the following based on the above passage:
   1. What is a pirate? (5)
   2. What sea was the most famous haunt of all for pirates? (5)
   3. Who was Grace O'Malley? (5)
   4. Where in the world today do pirates attack merchant ships? (5)

B. What are the ideal conditions that help pirates to carry out their attacks? (10)

C. What differences are there in the images of pirates which we get from stories and those which we get from films? (10)

D. Why do pirates still flourish today? (10)

E. Explain any **TWO** of the following in your own words:
   1. They have flourished for thousands of years (paragraph 1)
   2. Well-groomed hair (paragraph 3)
   3. The world of the pirate has almost always been exclusively male (paragraph 4)
   4. Speed is the principal tactic (paragraph 5) (10)

Practice question 2

The Wonders of the Modern World (Junior Certificate Ordinary Level 2007)

In 200 B.C. a list was made of the most impressive and beautiful man-made objects in the world. These were called 'The Seven Wonders of the World'. They were all statues or buildings such as the Pyramids of Egypt. In our time, there have been remarkable technical and scientific achievements, too. These achievements are so extraordinary that they deserve to be called the Wonders of the Modern World. Here are seven of these modern wonders:

1. **Computers:** They have already revolutionised the way we live, work, play and communicate. Even so, it is still early days for computers and every week we hear of new developments.

2. **Space Travel:** In 1969 an American astronaut, Neil Armstrong, stepped out of his space capsule onto the moon's surface and made his famous statement: 'That's one small step for a man, one giant leap for mankind.' Now anybody can enjoy a short trip into space. The only problem is that it costs several million euro!

3. **Medical Science:** Surely nothing has done more for the comfort and happiness of people than the advance of medical knowledge! How many million people have benefited from the humble aspirin? How many lives have been saved by antibiotics? Over the last hundred years average life expectancy has risen dramatically from about 50 in 1907 to about 75 today – all thanks to medical science.

4. **Holidays:** Yes – holidays! In fact there have always been holidays. Two thousand years ago in Ancient Rome, there were more than one hundred and fifty holidays a year. But a holiday simply meant a day off from work. One hundred years ago, only the very rich could travel abroad. Now, holiday makers from all walks of life travel to all parts of the world.

5. **The Olympic Games:** It is certainly true that the Olympic Games are now highly commercialised. Nevertheless, every country in the world takes part in them. Every four years for a short period, we see these countries come together in peace and friendship and we can feel hope again for the future of mankind.

6. **Agriculture:** In 1724 the famous Irish writer Jonathan Swift wrote: 'Whoever makes two blades of grass or two ears of corn grow where only one grew before

serves mankind better than the whole race of politicians.' In Europe, farmers have done this, thanks to scientific approaches to farming and to the development of new machinery. Today, we cannot eat all the food we produce. If only a way could be found to share this surplus food with those parts of the world where there is still famine!

7. **We are still here:** The last wonder of the modern world is simply that we are still here. There are all sorts of weapons of mass destruction that could destroy the population of the world, but these have not been used – yet! This is surely the greatest wonder of all.

Source: Adapted from *Wonders of the Modern World* by Ann Halliday

Questions

A. Find answers to the following questions based on the above passage:
   1. According to the passage, what list was made in 200 B.C.? (5)
   2. What did a 'holiday' mean in Ancient Rome? (5)
   3. According to the writer, what problem is associated with the Olympic Games? (5)
   4. Who, according to Jonathan Swift, does more for people than politicians? (5)

B. According to the passage, what is the chief difference between the Wonders of the Modern World and those of the Ancient World? (10)

C. Explain any **TWO** of the following in your own words:
   1. It is still early days (paragraph 1)
   2. One giant leap for mankind (paragraph 2)
   3 Average life expectancy (paragraph 3)
   4. Holiday makers from all walks of life (paragraph 4) (10)

D. In your opinion, which one of the seven wonders of the modern world is the most important? Give a reason for your answer. (10)

E. Choose a wonder of the modern world that you would add to the list given above. Explain why you would add this wonder. (10)

2 Personal Writing

- To examine the choices on the paper.
- To enable you to choose your essay wisely.
- To allow you to plan and write your essay.

Personal writing means **your essay or story**. In this section you will be asked to write an essay on one of the given topics. You will be given a wide choice and it is up to you to decide which topic you will write on. This is your opportunity to gain marks. You don't need any skills other than the ability to write.

This section, as with all the others, is worth **60 marks**. It will be difficult during the exam to manage your time well so **don't waste time** writing a very long essay. Regardless of how much you write, the maximum amount of marks available is 60 marks.

To gain full marks your essay should be **at least one page** (A4) of your answer book but **not longer than three pages**.

The choices

In the exam you will be given a list of approximately **eight choices**. This list will usually include:

- Short stories.
- Descriptive essays.
- Your thoughts on a topic.
- A dialogue or interview.

Most students look at the exam paper, see a title they think they could write about, pick up their pen and start writing. After the first paragraph (if they have remembered to use paragraphs) they stop writing to decide what they are going to write next, stare into space for ten minutes and then get worried that they are going to run out of time. So they hurriedly jot down an ending for their

Marks are awarded for:

- **Content:** The ideas and the originality of your essay.
- **Expression:** The words you use and how well you use them.
- **Structure:** Your use of paragraphs, beginning-middle-end and a logical structure in your essay.
- **Mechanics:** Spelling, grammar and punctuation.

story that probably doesn't make sense (such as a sudden ambush by terrorists) or turn to the old reliable ending, 'He woke up to find it was all a dream!'

If this describes the way your essays usually end up, **take a few moments now to consider your options.**

 **Option 1**: Keep writing your essays as you have always done and throw away key marks in your exam.	 **Option 2**: Take a few minutes to prepare for this section of the exam.

Choice 1: The short story

Read the choices on the exam paper carefully and make your choice. As most people write a short story in the exam, we will look at that choice first.

Step 1: Making the right choice for you

If you decide to write a story, here are some things you should keep in mind. In a short story the examiner is looking out for:

A: Plot.
B: Characters.
C: Setting.

A: Plot

The story should have a beginning, a middle and an end. These should make sense and should be **original**. That means that rather than trying to summarise the film you saw last weekend in two pages, you would be better off writing about what you know and making up your own story.

Your essay does not have to be a story: It is actually very difficult to write a well-structured story in 25 minutes under the pressure and stress of exam conditions.

There are other options on the paper: A dialogue or your thoughts on a topic are much easier to write under the time limits and you don't have to worry about how it is going to end, as those points will be outlined on the paper.

You can use an essay you have prepared earlier: Throughout the school year, you will be asked by your teacher to write essays. See if there is one that was actually quite good and check if you could adapt the titles in the exam to suit your essay.

B: Characters

Good stories have believable characters that are well described to the reader. This means that you shouldn't write a list of names or a list of characteristics, but rather **describe** your characters.

Don't just give a boring list that sounds like a police description, for example: Me and Tim and Carol and Alice and Erica went into town on the bus. Tim was tall and thin, Carol was blonde and tall, Alice was short and had brown hair and Erica was tall as well.	**Do** vary your sentences and include relevant details, for example: It was a bright sunny day so some of my friends and I decided we would go into town on the bus. As usual, Erica and Carol were late and Tim and Alice were going to leave without them. Tim was always a bit short tempered, but Alice kept him calm.

C: Setting

A story can be set in any time or place you wish, but try to bring the reader into the story by describing the place early on. You could describe the houses or clothing of the characters or give descriptions of the locality. Remember to use **adjectives** or describing words to create a sense of atmosphere. Read the example below and see how the author develops the setting and atmosphere.

Fly, Cherokee, Fly

It started like this: me and Garry Taylor were playing football in the park. I was in goal. On the night I found Cherokee, the ball had rolled up to the hedgerows near the bowling greens. And there she was, my special pigeon, hiding in the leaf mould under a hedge.

I crouched down slowly. Cherokee was sitting like a nesting bird, but I couldn't see any sign of eggs. She didn't look well. Her breast was puffed out as if she was cold and her feathers looked dull and broken in places. I pushed my hands forward to pick her up. She made a wooing noise and cocked her head. Her copper eye blinked and she tried to stand. 'I won't hurt you,' I whispered, and closed my hands around her. She stretched a pink foot out, but she didn't struggle.

Source: Adapted from *Fly, Cherokee, Fly* by Chris d'Lacey

exam focus

Direct speech (what people actually say in quotation marks) is very valuable in an essay. It shows us what type of people the characters are and moves the story along. But the key to using direct speech well is to use it sparingly and to keep the sentences short.

Try to use direct speech in your essays, but ask yourself two questions first:

1. Does it reveal something about the characters?
2. Does it move the story along?

If not don't use it!
Also, check your punctuation and make sure you **use quotation marks correctly.**

Step 2: Plan

In the exam, your plan could actually be quite **short** – just a few notes jotted down reminding you what you want to say in your essay, what should go into each paragraph and how it is going to end.

The most important function of the plan is to stop you from rambling all over the place and to keep you focused on what you want to say. So make sure you keep checking your plan while you are writing your essay to make sure you are still on track.

Once you decide on the title you wish to write about, you should jot down your ideas. When you organise your ideas into a sequence, this is your plan. Don't spend any longer than **three or four minutes** on your plan as you won't have enough time to write your essay otherwise.

You can write your plan either as a list or as a spider diagram.

In a spider diagram you write the title of your essay in the centre of your page and jot down your ideas around it.

You can then number your ideas to decide in what order you will write them and get rid of any ideas you no longer wish to use.

Once you have decided on your sequence, with a beginning, middle and end, you can start writing.

One thing you need to keep in mind is to **KEEP IT SIMPLE!** You have 25 minutes to write a story. Stick to describing **one** event with **two** or **three** characters. If you allow your story to be more complicated than that, you will not get it written in the time given.

Sample Plan: Spider diagram

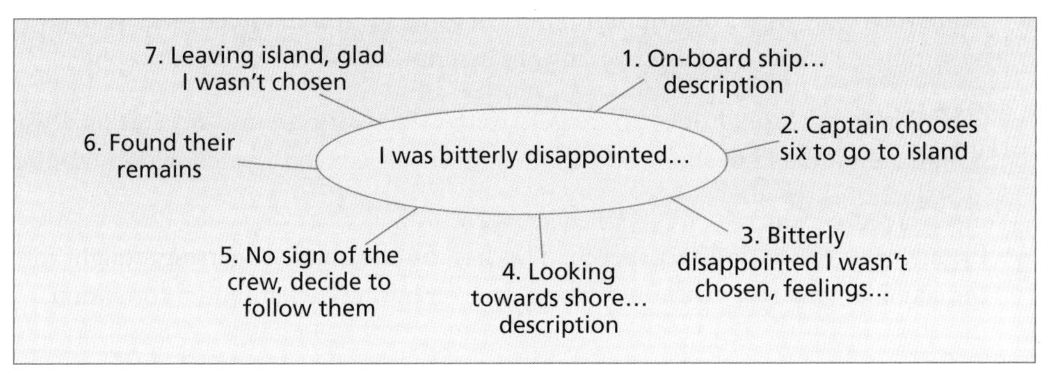

Step 3: Starting to write

It might sound basic, but writing a good essay depends on two things: sentences and paragraphs.

Sentences: Make sure you use **capital letters** at the beginning of your sentences and **full stops** at the end. Try to keep your sentences to the point and **break down long sentences** into two or three shorter ones. It will help your essay make more sense. Don't keep writing phrases like 'and then..., and then...' This just makes your essay sound repetitive and boring.

Paragraphs: Use paragraphs in your essay to divide up your story. Every time something new happens you should start a new paragraph. Each paragraph should begin slightly in from the edge of the page. This will make your essay look much neater and more structured.

Short sentences that are correct and make sense will gain more marks than one long sentence that takes up an entire paragraph.

Try to avoid some common mistakes:

Don't begin with a list: 'John and Tony and Sam and Frank went to the circus. They met Ed and George and Sylvia when they got there.' This type of opening sentence is just boring!

Don't give ridiculous detail: 'At 8.45 they left for school. At 8.56 they got to school. They went to their first class until 9.40 and then had double P.E. until 11.00. At break time they each had two chocolate bars and a can of coke.' This type of information doesn't add anything to the story – it just makes it dull.

Do start when your story starts: 'John and Jason were brothers. They went to the same school and had lots of the same friends. John was ten and Jason was twelve. John liked football but Jason liked basketball. They had a dog and a cat. The brothers ... basketball match ...' Some students tend to write a lot of background information at the beginning of their story. This just prevents your story from getting started, especially if none of the information given is important to the story. Get stuck into your story and reveal the important information as it is needed.

The opening paragraph

You should try to **grab the reader's attention** right from the opening lines of your story. There are some easy ways to draw the reader in:

- Begin your essay with a **description**. This will bring the reader directly into your story by setting the scene. Use adjectives in your description to help create atmosphere.

  'The wind cut through me. My fingers were frozen stiff around my hurley. I was standing in midfield in shorts and thick woollen socks. God I hated winter training sessions.'

- Begin your story with **direct speech**. This has the advantage of getting straight into the action of your story without wasting time on boring background information.

'"Go on Jack, grab it!" The shouts of the boys below made me forget about the twenty-foot drop to the ground.'

- Use **suspense**. Don't reveal everything in the first sentence. Keep the reader guessing, as this will also keep them interested.

'He walked slowly out of the shop. Maybe they hadn't seen his face. Maybe. He quickened his footsteps until he reached the corner. Then he broke into a run.'

The body of your story

Try to make your story as interesting as possible but also keep it **believable**! Your story should be between **six and eight paragraphs**. Try not to race to the end but describe each step along the way. Use adjectives in your descriptions and try to describe the sounds and smells of a scene, not just the sights.

Conclusion

The end of your story, or conclusion, should be **logical**. Don't say something like 'and then I woke up' at the end. If you have planned it, you should know how it is going to end. Don't feel that you have to tie up all the loose ends. You are writing your story in 25 minutes, so don't have a very complicated story with lots of information filled in at the end.

Practice questions

Keeping the above points in mind, try writing a plan for each of the following essays. Try to write some of them fully and make the opening paragraphs as interesting as possible.

1. The day that our cat or dog began to talk. (2008)
2. The first time I met him/her. (2009)
3. Write a story which at some point includes the sentence: 'You should have seen the look on his/her face...' (2009)
4. Write a story about an old lady or an old man. (2004)
5. '"Do not go outside! Do not go outside! Close all windows and doors..." The message was repeated over and over again, on all T.V. and radio stations.' Continue the story. (2003)
6. Look at the accompanying photograph. It is a famous painting by the artist Munch, called 'The Scream'. Write the story which you imagine gave rise to this painting.

So far we have looked at writing a short story, but there are other choices on the paper. For most people the other choices are much easier to write than a short story. That means that you can gain more marks by trying a different type of essay, so let's look at some of the other choices.

Choice 2: The descriptive essay

In this type of essay you are asked to give a description of an event, person or place.

Step 1: Making the right choice for you

You do **not** have to write a story for this type of essay. It can be just a description. **No characters or plot** - just describing something. So if you like writing descriptions but when you write a story you find the plot difficult, then this could be the choice for you. **But you still need a plan!** If you don't plan, then you may write a very boring, repetitive essay.

Step 2: Plan

It is very easy to prepare for this type of essay. Think about something you could write a lot about: a club you are involved in? A hobby you have? Your experiences in school? Your family? A typical holiday? An elderly relative?
Jot down all your ideas about this topic. Use headings to sort out your thoughts. Think about the sights, sounds, smells and feelings associated with your topic.

Think about your title. Jot down anything that springs to mind. Use the following headings to help you gather your ideas:
Sights: What things do you usually see? People? How are they dressed? Perhaps you notice animals, buildings, trees or flowers more than people?
Sounds: What do you usually hear? Machinery? Talking? Shouting? Laughing?
Smells: What do you usually smell? Nice smells? Unpleasant smells?
Touch: What can you feel? Cold? Warmth? Pain?
Feel: What do you feel? Fearful? Nervous? Excited? Happy?
Taste: What does the food taste like? Bitter? Sweet?

exam TIPS

Note: You could also use these headings to improve your descriptions in short stories.

Sample plan

Describe a trip to a funfair.

- **Sights:** Neon lights, sawdust, Ferris wheel, ticket sellers, stalls, families in groups, crowds of children, shoot the duck, throwing rings, roller coaster, ghost train.
- **Sounds:** Screams of laughter, shouts of sellers: 'Roll up! Roll up!', crying children, clatter of train on track, tinny music, crashes of bumper cars.

- **Smells:** Candy floss, children getting sick, popcorn, oil from machinery, chips.
- **Touch:** Goosebumps of excitement, shiver from gust of wind at the top of the Ferris wheel, butterflies of nervousness in stomach.
- **Feel:** Excitement, nervous, happy, anticipation.
- **Taste:** Salt and vinegar tang of the chips, melt in your mouth sweetness of candy floss.

Step 3: Starting to write

Using your list, add adjectives to the words. Rather than just saying 'The house was old' you could add **adjectives** and say 'The crumbling old house'. Use all your senses to describe the scene. 'The crumbling old house had a faint musty smell.'

If you are describing an event, start at the beginning and use your plan to describe each aspect of the event.

You may also be asked to write a descriptive essay on a person rather than an event or a place. Read the following descriptions of people and identify the techniques the writers use to bring their descriptions to life.

'That man is like a cockroach,' Phillis commented. 'Stamp on him and he'll just come out somewhere else.'
The description was apt. He even looked like a cockroach, especially from the back. His shiny cap of greased brown hair emerged from his long rusty coat which was split like a wing case and stuck out over his polished-booted legs. Her description made me laugh out loud.
Source: *Pirates* by Celia Rees

For the thousandth time, Meg Finn wondered what she was doing here. How had she sunk this far – skulking around the granny flats with a lowlife like Belch Brennan? Her reflection glared accusingly from the window pane. For a second she saw the ghost of her mother in that face. The same wide blue eyes, the same braided blonde hair, even the same frown wrinkles between her eyebrows. What would Mam think of this latest escapade? Meg's involuntary blush answered the question for her.
Source: *The Wish List* by Eoin Colfer

Practice questions

Using the following titles, try to write a descriptive essay.

1. Travelling on the school bus. (2005)
2. 'And the winners are...' Describe a competition in which your class or your school or your club has taken part. (2005)
3. The best time of the day. (2005)
4. My dream job. (2009)
5. My favourite leisure time activity. (2004)
6. Thoughts in a traffic jam. (2003)
7. Living in the city or in the country. (2007)

Choice 3: Your thoughts on a topic

In the exam you may be asked to give your thoughts on an issue or subject.

- The aim in this essay is to be as **sincere** as possible. You are **not** writing a fictional story so it would probably be best if you don't plan to start a nuclear war if you were Taoiseach.
- **Be aware of your audience**. You are writing this as part of an exam that will be corrected by teachers, so don't write an entire essay about how dreadful you think teachers are.
- You should try to cover different areas in your essay so think about the different headings you could use in your plan. For example, in an essay where you write about what you would do if you were Taoiseach, you might look at what you would do in areas such as education, health care, local amenities and sport.

Step 1: Making the right choice for you

If you have strong opinions and like to debate issues then this choice may be for you.

The titles will usually allow you write at length about your chosen topic. While these seem to be very straightforward, you need to remember the following:

- You still need to **plan** your essay. Don't run the risk of writing all you want to say in the first paragraph.
- Your essay still needs to be at least one A4 page.

Step 2: Plan

Use headings in your plan to expand your thoughts and ideas on a topic. For example, a plan for the essay 'If I were Taoiseach...' might look like this:

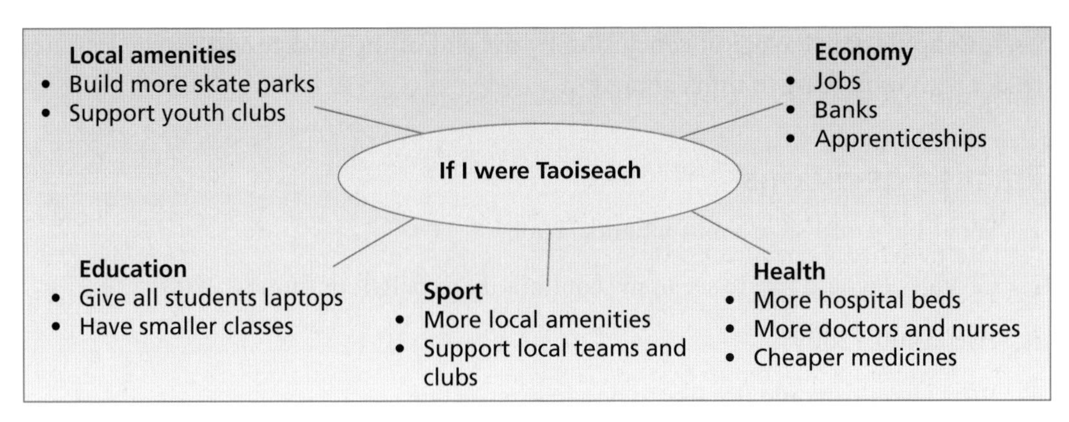

Read the following passage and identify how the writer puts across his opinion on the subject.

Online shopping

I am never going to buy anything electrical from a high street shop again. From now on it's strictly online shopping for me. This stems from a growing realisation that technology has run well ahead of virtually anybody who works in these shops.

Some time ago, when shopping for components for a home wireless network, I was chatting with a sales assistant about the different pieces of kit when a thought struck me. I asked him, 'You haven't got a clue what I am talking about, have you?' A little direct perhaps but the chap replied quite cheerfully, 'No, I haven't.'

Funnily enough, I think the shops themselves have begun to realise that technology itself is changing the way we shop. A lot of people now do their research online before they make a visit to a store. This is why, for those who do a lot of research, they tend to know more about the products than the people who sell them.

This is having huge consequences, and it's not just about the physical goods: we can, for example, access the opinions of thousands of other people about the quality of just about any hotel in the world. This means rip-offs have become less common in a world of free information.

Just how any bog-standard retailer is supposed to be able to make money in such a world is beyond me.

Source: Adapted from Chris Johns, *The Irish Times*, 3 May 2006

Step 3: Starting to write

If you examine the above passage, you will notice that the **writer gives his opinion from the very beginning** of the passage. **He starts with a statement and then explains why he has reached this conclusion**. You can use this structure in your essay. Be very clear about what you want to say and support your opinion throughout your essay.

You should reach a logical conclusion by the end of the passage and maybe leave the reader with something to think about.

Practice questions

1. What I like or dislike about Ireland. (2008)
2. Changes I would like to see in my community or neighbourhood. (2008)
3. Friendship. (2009)
4. Why I would/would not like to be a teacher. (2008)
5. If I were principal in our school... (2002)
6. Things that really frighten me. (2009)

Choice 4: Dialogue or interview

You may be asked to write your essay in the form of a dialogue or interview. This is a relatively easy option as the question usually tells you what you need to write about and the structure is very straightforward.

While writing a dialogue you do **not** need to worry about using quotation marks or inverted commas. Your dialogue should be written as follows:

Pat: James! How are you doing today?
James: Never better Pat, never better!

An interview would follow the same format, with the questions and answers each starting on a new line.

Be aware of the following:

- Your characters' names should be on the **left-hand side of the page** followed by a **colon (:).**
- You **don't** need to use inverted commas (‘’).
- You can include background information at the beginning of your piece.
- You can include directions about what the characters should do or how they would say a line. This should be placed in brackets after the character's name.
- You still need to use other punctuation, such as full stops and question marks.
- Keep your dialogue realistic and interesting.
- Allow yourself space to lay out your dialogue clearly.

Sample:

Q: So, Brad, what are your plans for the future?
A: At present I am quite busy at home with the kids, but I'm always reading new scripts!

Practice questions

1. 'Why can't I go? Everyone else is...' Write a composition which includes the above sentences. (2008)
2. 'You can't go out wearing that!' Write an essay that includes the above sentence. (2007)
3. Write out the conversation which might take place between any two rubbish items. (2003)

Other choices

There may be another choice on the paper that you have not seen before. You may be given a **picture** to use as a starting point for a story or you may be asked to write a **diary entry** as a particular character or something completely different. Don't panic. The examiner is always looking for the same thing in your writing:

- Good content – an original story.
- Good expression – words used well.
- Good structure – evidence of planning.

So take your time and make the right choice for you in the exam. Plan your answer. If you have time, reread your essay and correct any mistakes.

3 Functional Writing

- To understand the tasks set in the exam.
- To write according to the task.

This section of the paper must be answered and is worth **60 marks**. You are usually given **two choices** of which you have to answer one. The aim of this section is to write **according to the task** required.

Make sure you read the question carefully and you know **exactly** what you are asked to do. The choices in the exam can be broken down into the following categories:

1. Informal or personal letter.
2. Formal letter.
3. Speech.
4. Report.
5. Instructions, rules and codes.
6. Review or blurb.
7. Description of a photograph.

exam TIPS

The language used should be **formal** so avoid using slang, abbreviations or text spelling.

As this section is worth the same amount of marks as every other section in your exam, don't think you can get away with writing half a page. **Your answer should be at least one page of your answer book.** Use the space given to make your answer look neat, especially when you are writing a letter. **Presentation** is important, as it helps you to communicate with the examiner and it is your skill in communicating that is being tested in this section.

1. Informal letter

This is the type of letter that you would send to a **friend** or someone that is **known personally** to you. It is important to be aware of the **layout** and punctuation, as there are marks awarded for these.

The **tone** and language used should be **friendly** and it should be obvious that you know this person well.

ɜreeting: In an ɴformal letter ɦe greeting ɦould be **ɘersonal** and ɦould be just the ɪrst name of the ɘerson you are ʋriting to.

ɅAain part of ɘtter: Your letter ɦould be ersonal, so don't ɔrget to ask ɥuestions ɦroughout. You ɘed to break ɔwn your letter ɪto **paragraphs**, ɔ each time you art a new topic ɔu should start a ɘw paragraph.

ɡn off: Several ɾsions are ɕceptable: Your ɘnd, All my ɤe, See you ɔn, etc. Just ake sure that e first letter of e first word is a ɒpital letter.

Date: This can be written in various forms: 20 May '13, 20-05-13, 20/05/13.

62 Orchard Park,
Athy,
Co. Kildare.

20 May 2013

Your address: This should be written at the **top right-hand** corner of the page. Make sure you leave enough space to fit each line of the address on a separate line. Each line of the address begins with a capital letter and is followed by a comma, except the last one which has a full stop.

Dear Jack,

____
____
______________________________?
____
____
______________________________?
____
____
____
____
____
____
____
____
_______________.

Your friend,

Kate

Signature

Make sure you answer the question asked. To make sure you stick to the point, a brief plan is useful.

Sample question

Write a letter to a friend you met while on holidays in Spain during the summer. In your letter you should:

- Tell them about your summer since you returned.
- Ask them to visit you in the future.
- Outline some activities you could plan for the visit.

Sample answer

25 Ash Drive,
Newcastlewest,
Co. Limerick.
30-07-11

Dear Sarah,
How's life with you? Did you get back OK? Our flight was delayed for two hours on the way back so we had to sit around the airport for ages! Plus it was 2.00 am, so none of the shops were open! But we got back eventually, safe and sound.

Did you hear from Pedro since you got back? He did say he would send you an e-mail, but then Anthony said the same to me and I haven't heard a thing from him!

What are you doing for the rest of the summer? Would you like to come and visit and stay with us for a week? I know we won't have the same weather we had in Spain but I'm sure we could find something to keep us amused!! There is a big Munster match on next month that I am definitely going to, so that could be fun. My Dad has also promised to bring me shopping in Limerick, so we could do that when you get here.

I hope you can come down soon. Looking forward to hearing from you!
Your friend,
Jessica

Practice questions

1. You are in the Gaeltacht for four weeks. Write a letter home to your parents describing your experiences.
2. Write a letter to your aunt thanking her for the Christmas present she sent you.
3. Write a letter to your best friend who is in hospital. Tell them about things that they have missed in the past week.
4. Write a letter to the *Milan Messenger*, an Italian newspaper, in the hope of finding an Italian pen pal. In your letter, introduce yourself in some detail. Also explain why you are interested in corresponding with an Italian pen pal. (2004)
5. Recently, during a party in a friend's house, you dropped a plate of greasy chips and tomato ketchup on the sofa and carpet. Write a letter of apology to your friend's parents. You should:
   - Introduce yourself.
   - Explain what happened.
   - Apologise.
   - Offer to help. (2007)

2. Formal letter

You may be asked to write a letter in which formal language is used. These letters are written to people you **don't know personally**. You may be asked to apply for a job or to complain about the service in a restaurant, for example. The **structure** of a formal letter is slightly different to that of an informal letter.

The **language** used in these letters is very **polite and serious**. Never use slang or abbreviations.

he address of he person you re writing to hould be written n the left-hand de of the page n the line below e date. You hould include e name and tle of the person u are writing to you know it.

Your address and date should be written as before.

68 John Street,
Tullow,
Co. Carlow.
26-05-13

The Manager,
The Salon,
Main Street,
Tullow,
Co. Carlow.

Dear Sir or Madam,

reeting: If you now the name f the person you e writing to, u should ddress them ersonally, e.g. ear Mr Jones. ever use their rst name, as this unds too formal. If you n't know the me, then you ould address e letter to 'Dear or Madam' or whom it may ncern'.

Main body of the letter: Your letter should be divided into **paragraphs**. Usually two or three paragraphs are enough. Make sure you **stick to the point** in your letter and answer what is being asked in the question.

Yours faithfully,

Closing: If you have named the person you are writing to, you should end with 'Yours sincerely'. If not, then you should use 'Yours faithfully'.

nature

John Smith

Sample question

Write a letter to a local restaurant where you have received poor service and poor quality food.

Sample answer

62 The Terrace,
Newbridge,
Co. Kildare.

13-05-13

Mr S. Smith,
The Manager,
The Red Lobster,
Main Street,
Newbridge,
Co. Kildare.

Dear Mr Smith,

I attended a dinner party in your restaurant on Friday May 10th. I, along with seven other guests, had made a reservation for 7.30 p.m. to celebrate the birthday of my brother. Your staff assured me that this would be no problem.

From the very beginning of the evening there seemed to be no end of problems. Our reservation had been overlooked and we had to wait for an hour for another table to become available. Our waitress was rude and failed to deliver any of the correct orders. The dish my brother ordered, the duck, was overcooked and inedible. The cake we had brought was hacked to pieces and the coffee was cold.

Overall the evening was a very unpleasant experience and ruined my brother's birthday celebration. I expect, at the very least, an apology for the way we were treated and I hope the situation can be rectified to everyone's satisfaction.

Yours sincerely,

Mr Jack Fletcher

- Stick to the point and answer all parts of the question.
- Use formal, serious language.
- Use paragraphs.
- Use the space given and lay out your answer neatly.

Practice questions

1. You are a resident in a locality affected by the dumping of rubbish. Write a letter to your local county council or corporation. In it you should:
   - Describe the problem.
   - State your annoyance.
   - Make suggestions for dealing with the situation. (2003)
2. Your class decides to raise funds for local charities. You plan to hold a photography competition in your school. Write a letter to the school principal. In your letter you could:
   - Ask for the use of the hall.
   - Explain the purpose of the competition.
   - Describe how you will organise it.
   - Tell how you will advertise it. (2001)
3. Write a letter of application for **ONE** of the following summer jobs:
   - Waitress/waiter.
   - Car wash attendant.
   - Child minder.
   - Dog walker. (2009)

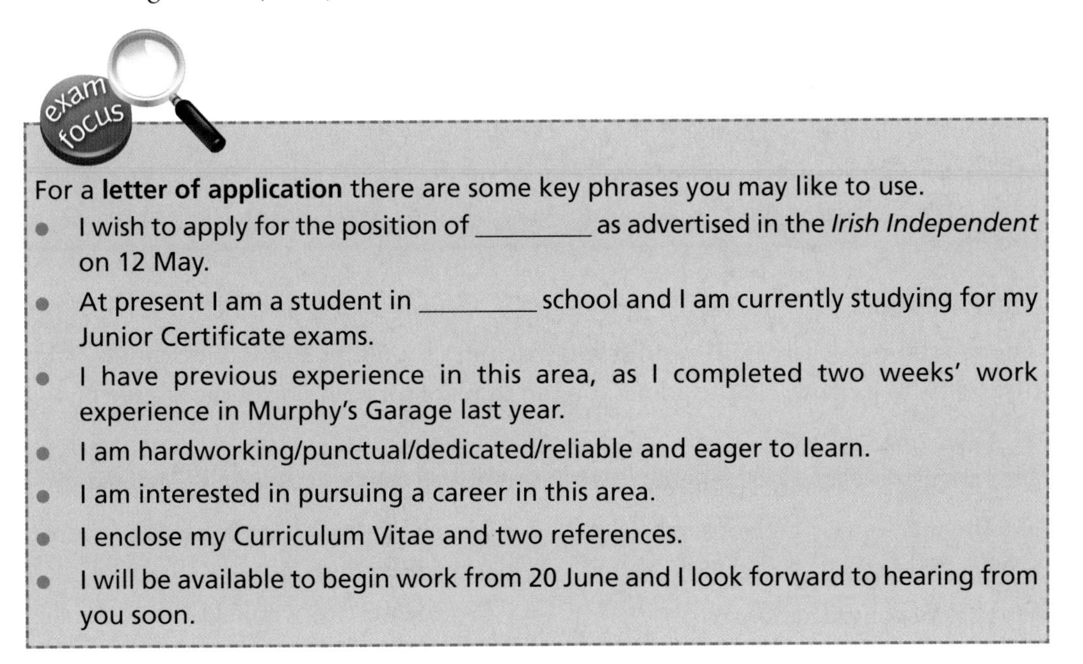

For a **letter of application** there are some key phrases you may like to use.

- I wish to apply for the position of ________ as advertised in the *Irish Independent* on 12 May.
- At present I am a student in ________ school and I am currently studying for my Junior Certificate exams.
- I have previous experience in this area, as I completed two weeks' work experience in Murphy's Garage last year.
- I am hardworking/punctual/dedicated/reliable and eager to learn.
- I am interested in pursuing a career in this area.
- I enclose my Curriculum Vitae and two references.
- I will be available to begin work from 20 June and I look forward to hearing from you soon.

3. Speech

The aim of a debate speech is to **persuade** the audience that your argument is correct. To do this you should **support your points** using examples, facts and logical argument.

A common question in the Junior Certificate exam is to write a debate speech. In this question you are asked to **support one side or another of an argument or motion.** The motion will be stated on the paper.

Writing a debate speech is not difficult. Just as with writing the formal letter, there are a few **key phrases** that will help you structure your answer.

- **Step 1 – Plan:** Jot down a few ideas for both sides of the argument. See which side of the argument you can write more about and focus on that.
- **Step 2 – Support:** For every point you make you should be able to support it. Think about examples from books, television, news, etc. that support your side of the argument.
- **Step 3 – Write:** Use the sample introduction below to write your first paragraph. **Each point you make and the support for that point should be in separate paragraphs.** Use the conclusion below to write your own conclusion.

Overall, your speech should be a minimum of one A4 page.

Write a speech **for** or **against** the motion that 'all soft drinks machines should be banned in schools'.

You should be either totally **for** or totally **against** this motion. State clearly and convincingly the reasons for your point of view. (2005)

Step 1: Plan

The motion for debate is 'All soft drinks machines should be banned in schools.' Your first step is to jot down all the points you can think of for each side of the argument.

For

- Unhealthy for school children.
- Too much sugar, bad for teeth.
- Sugar rush, hyperactive children.
- Lack of concentration.
- Too expensive.

Against

- Provides necessary liquids after P.E.
- Money generated can be used by school to provide equipment.
- Provides service, would just go to the shop anyway.

You then need to decide which side of the debate you will write on. It is probably easier to write an argument *supporting* the motion, that is, saying that all soft drinks machines

should be banned in schools as you have more points for this side of the argument. So you have taken your first step, deciding whether you are for or against the motion.

Remember this is an English exam, not a court of law, so it is perfectly acceptable to make up your own facts and figures. Try to keep them believable, though!

Step 2: Support

To support your points you could **outline facts and figures.** In this case you could talk about obesity levels in children. You could look at the situation in other countries to support your points and you could use your own personal experience.

Step 3: Write

- **First Paragraph:** This is similar for all debate speeches. Look at the example below and adapt it to suit the speech you are writing.
- **Second Paragraph:** You can **define the motion**. Outline or explain some parts of the motion. For example in the above motion you don't want to exclude bottled water vending machines. Focus on the fact that the motion states soft drinks machines. You could also **outline your argument.**
- **Third, fourth and fifth paragraphs**: Here you make your point, explain your point and support your point. Use facts, statistics or personal examples to support your point.
- **Last paragraph:** You should **sum up** your points and state again what side of the argument you are on. Look at the sample below for ideas.

Sample speech

troduction: ate which side the motion u are on.

Chairperson, adjudicators, members of the opposition, friends: We are here today to debate the motion that 'all soft drinks machines should be banned in schools'. **My team mates and I totally support this motion.**

We, of course, totally support the bottled water vending machines or healthy drinks machines that can be found in some schools. But this motion singles out soft drinks machines, and it is this type of vending machine that my team mates and I are totally against.

ch point gets a ragraph and is oported.

It has been proven again and again that these soft drinks are **full of sugar** and have a severe effect on young children. You only have to look at the effect soft drinks have at a children's party to realise that this can't be good. Drinking soft drinks during the day can lead to children being hyperactive.

This obviously is not a state to be in when you are supposed to be learning. This in turn leads to disruptive behaviour in classrooms and can cause discipline problems for staff and pupils.

Use **questions** to persuade the audience.

You only have to look at the **rising levels of obesity** in children in the United States to see what will happen here if we continue to allow these machines in our schools. **Surely you do not want this to happen?**

Lastly, the enormous **cost of these drinks machines** can place too much **pressure** on children and parents to have a steady supply of cash to feed into the drinks machine. And who benefits from these machines? Certainly not the children.

Closing: sums up your argument

For all of these reasons, the disruptive effect on school life, the negative effects on the health of the children involved and the ridiculous expense of these machines, my team mates and I strongly feel that you should join with us in supporting this motion that 'all soft drinks machines should be banned in schools'.

Thank you.

Remember you are writing for an **audience**. Your first paragraph must **address the audience** you are speaking to. Use the introductory paragraph above as a guideline for writing your opening paragraph.

In the second paragraph you can define your motion. This means you **highlight the areas you want to focus on** and can **get rid of some of the points that may be used against you**. In the example the second paragraph excluded water vending machines from the argument and focused on the soft drinks machines in the motion. This made the argument easier to make.

You are trying to **persuade** the audience, so try to win them over to your side by using some of the following **techniques**:

- Use obvious questions (**rhetorical questions**). Look at the example above. The question, 'Surely you do not want this to happen?' is a rhetorical question. It makes the audience feel they would be right to support your argument.
- **Use examples that everyone can relate to**. In the example above the reference to children's parties is used. Everyone knows what these can be like and so can relate to the point you are trying to make.

In the final paragraph sum up the points you have made and state again the side of the motion you are on. Finally, **thank** the audience for listening.

Practice questions

1. Write out your argument for or against the motion that 'Footballers or top models or pop stars are paid too much.' (2003)
2. The motion for debate is 'Teenagers today are too easily influenced by celebrities'. Write out your speech in full. (2008)
3. You are taking part in a debate. The motion for debate is 'Full driving licences should not be issued to people under twenty'. You need to:
   - Decide whether you are for or against the motion.
   - Think about the points you are going to make.
   - Plan the order in which you will make them.
   - Now write your speech in full. (2007)
4. Write a speech for or against the motion that 'Teenagers should be called "screenagers" because they are addicted to screens – T.V., phones, electronic games...' You need to:
   - Decide whether you are for or against the motion.
   - Think about the points you are going to make.
   - Plan the order in which you will make them.
   - Now write out the speech in full. (2009)

4. Report

There are **two types** of reports you may be asked to write:

- A news report or article.
- A report on an issue.

News report

A news report for a newspaper is a **factual** piece of writing. You are trying to tell the reader the important key points of the event and give your opinion on why it happened. Included in a report you could have **quotations** from eye witnesses and statements from those involved.

The **structure** of a report is generally as follows:

- Paragraph 1: Who? What? When? Where?
- Paragraph 2: Why?
- Paragraph 3: Quotes or statements.
- Paragraph 4: Outlook for the future.

You may also be asked to write a report on an **incident** you have witnessed. In this type of report, a similar structure may be followed. The important thing to remember is to include the key information: Who? What? When? Where? You may also include your **opinion** of why something happened but try to keep your report as **factual** as possible.

Sample question

Write a report for a newspaper on a traffic accident.

Sample answer

Car Crash Carnage

by John Smith

At approximately 6.15 this morning two cars collided on the main Dublin to Naas road. The two drivers and two other passengers were taken to Naas General Hospital and are said to be in a stable condition.

The icy road conditions may have led one of the drivers to lose control of their car and skid across the central barrier. The temperature last night reached a record low of -8°C and widespread black ice was reported in the area.

A local resident said they heard 'screeching of brakes and a loud bang' at the time reported. A Garda spokesman has said that the drivers will be questioned when they are released from hospital. It is uncertain yet if any charges will be brought against the drivers involved.

The stretch of road where the accident took place is known locally as an accident black spot, as four similar accidents have taken place there in the past six months. Residents have asked the Minister for Transport to begin a road improvement scheme that has been postponed three times so far. The minister was unavailable for comment.

Practice questions

1. You have witnessed an attempted bank robbery. Write out the report you would write for the Gardaí.
2. Write a report for your local newspaper on an important school match.
3. Write a report for your local paper on an issue that affects your area.

Report on an issue

This type of report is not for a newspaper but would be **given to a group or committee.** For example, you may be asked to write a report on proposals for a new school uniform by the principal.

When writing this type of report you could structure your answer around the following headings, but they may be changed as necessary:

- **Title:** What exactly is your report about? For example, it could be a report on proposals for a new school uniform.
- **Introduction:** Who asked for the report? Who wrote it? For example, as requested by the principal, carried out by the school council.
- **Research:** What research did you do? Did you carry out surveys? Who did you ask? What types of questions did you ask?
- **Results:** What were the results of the survey? Give percentages. List your findings without giving your opinion.
- **Conclusions:** What conclusions have you reached as a result of this survey? This is where you include your opinion based on the findings you have listed above.
- **Recommendations:** List three or four points that you recommend should happen.
- **Sign and date:** Sign and date the report on behalf of the group.

key point

You don't need to write very much under each of the headings and you can combine some of the sections as it suits you.

Sample question

Write a report on **proposals for a new school uniform**.

Sample answer

Title: Report on proposals for a new school uniform.

Introduction: As **requested by the principal**, carried out by the school council.

Research: We **surveyed a wide variety of people** to get a well-rounded view of what the new uniform should be. We asked a sample group of **students, parents and teachers.** The questions we asked **looked at all aspects of the uniform** and how suitable each new suggestion was.

Results:

- 90 per cent of those asked felt that a polo shirt option should be available for the summer months.
- 40 per cent of those asked felt that the girls should be allowed wear trousers as an alternative to a skirt, especially in winter.
- 60 per cent of students felt that students should be allowed to wear runners but 90 per cent of staff and parents said they should wear shoes.

- 20 per cent felt that no uniform should be worn.
- 75 per cent felt that the colours used at present were fine but that the quality of the jumpers could be better.

Conclusions: There are a lot of different opinions about the uniform. Regardless of what changes are made, some people will still be unhappy. There are some suggestions that most people agree on and these could be changed immediately.
Recommendations:

- A summer polo shirt should be ordered for the summer months in the school colours.
- More research needs to be done into the option of trousers for the girls.
- The school colours should remain the same but a new supplier should be found for the jumpers.

Signed:
The School Council
21-05-13

Practice questions

1. Write a report for your local town council about the problem of litter in your area.
2. Write a report for a holiday company on the disastrous holiday you had last summer. Outline the recommendations you would make so that no one else would have to have the same experience.

5. Instructions, rules and codes

Occasionally in the exam you may be asked to write a set of instructions or rules. The **language** you use here should be **clear** and **to the point**.

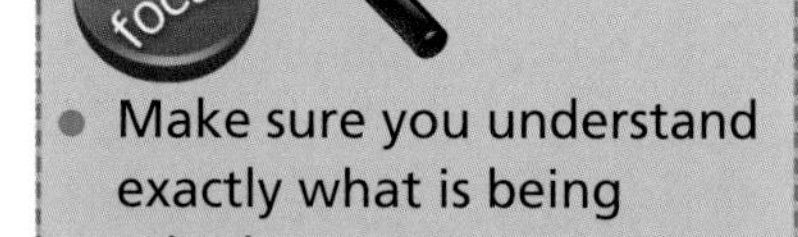

- Make sure you understand exactly what is being asked.
- Divide up your answer into **logical steps.**
- Keep your explanations short.
- When writing instructions, detail each logical step and explain any terms used.

Practice questions

1. Your class is making up a town or city code for your area. You have been chosen as class secretary. In *A Code for Our Town,* the class points out:
   - What should be done.
   - What should not be done.
   - Why.

Now, write *A Code for our Town* in full. (2002)

2. Write out the rules of a photography competition. In the rules you should mention:
   - The different groupings of pictures.
   - The different age groups involved.
   - The regulations about entries.
   - The prizes to be won. (2001)

3. Descriptions of games for teenagers are to be included in a millennium time capsule. You wish to contribute a description of a game you like. For future teenagers:
   - Describe how the game is played
   - List some of the main rules. (2000)

6. Review or blurb

A review is your opinion of a book, film, CD, etc. When you are writing a review, you should include the following:

- The full title of the film, book or CD along with the name of the director, author or band, etc.
- Possibly some background information.
- A **summary** of the book, CD or film – but don't give away the important parts such as the ending of the film.
- **Your opinion**. Highlight the high points and discuss the weaknesses but try to be balanced.
- If you liked it, you should be enthusiastic and encourage others to experience it.

A **blurb** is the written text on the back cover of a book or DVD. It usually contains an outline of the plot, gives details of the characters and/or the actors playing them and tries to promote the book or DVD.

The main purpose of a blurb is to sell the book or DVD, so it is always full of praise with no negative comments.

Sample review

Mission Impossible III

Directed by J.J. Abrams

Starring: Tom Cruise, Philip Seymour Hoffman, Ving Rhames, Michelle Monaghan
12A Cert

Starting the summer blockbuster season with a big bang, *Mission Impossible III* raises the bar for all the mega-budget action extravaganzas to follow in the weeks ahead. J.J. Abrams, making a start as a director after his experience on *Lost* and *Alias*, was an inspired choice to helm this adrenaline-pumping adventure.

Abrams ignores the Bond-like opening sequence that has seemed normal for the genre and immediately gets down to the business of heroes and villains as Owen Davian (Philip Seymour Hoffman) gives secret agent Ethan Hunt (Tom Cruise) a countdown to 10, during which he has to reveal the location of a rabbit's foot or a tied-up woman will die.

Hoffman makes Davian a formidable enemy, an unscrupulous, conscience-free black market trader in weapons and information, regardless of the human consequences.

The set-pieces are spectacular, as they need to be, and orchestrated with remarkable cinematic flair and exemplary stunt work. Crucially the movie gets its priorities right, in that its many special effects are there to serve the story, rather than the other way round. Abrams propels the action at such an accelerated pace that there's barely time to draw breath.

Source: Michael Dwyer, *The Irish Times*, 5 May 2006 (adapted)

Practice questions

1. Write a review of any TV drama series you watch regularly. In the review you might refer to:
   - The setting.
   - The main character.
   - The quality of the acting. (1997)

2. Write a review of a film you have seen recently. In your review you should include:
   - Name of the film.
   - A brief summary of the plot.
   - In your opinion, the high point of the film (actors? setting? special effects?).

3. Write the blurb for a DVD cover of a film you enjoyed.

7. Description of a photograph

You may be asked to write a detailed description of a photograph that will be presented with the paper. If you choose this option, you should keep the following points in mind:

- **State the obvious.** Say if the photograph is black and white or colour, if it is a landscape or a portrait of people, etc.
- Divide the photograph into sections and describe each one separately: 'In the **background** there is...', 'In the **middle ground** we see...', 'In the **foreground** there is...'.
- Describe the **expressions** on the faces of the **people** involved: 'He is smiling and looks relaxed and happy.'
- Describe the **atmosphere**: 'It looks dark and bleak because...', 'It looks happy and cheerful because...'.

Practice questions

1. Write accurate descriptions of the following photographs.

(a)

(b)

(c)

4 Fiction

- To prepare for the **unseen fiction** question.
- To prepare answers for the **studied fiction** question.

If the fiction section appears in section 4, then it is compulsory and you must answer the questions. If it appears in section 5, 6 or 7 you have a choice, as you have to answer just two of the three sections.

The **fiction** section has appeared most often in **Section 4** of the exam.

In the fiction section, you are asked to read an extract from a novel and answer the questions that follow. The last question will ask you about the novel or short stories you have studied and you will have to write two or three paragraphs on that novel or short story.

Unseen fiction

There are several types of questions asked on the unseen extract:

1. Comprehension questions

These questions ask if you understood the passage and require you to find information in the extract. In your answers to these questions, it is important that you do the following:

- Always use **full sentences**. For example, if asked what the main character's name is, you should say: 'The main character's name is John', rather than just answering 'John'.
- Answer **exactly** what the question is asking you. In fact, you should use the wording from the question in your answer to be sure that you are answering the question asked. For example, the question is: 'What did the character do when his mother returned?' Your answer should begin with the words 'When his mother returned he...'.
- Use **quotations** from the text to support your answer. Your quotes do not need to be long, just to the point.
- Sometimes, just one word from the passage is enough to support your point. For example: 'Hugh's mother insults Hugh when she says he is "almost" a man.'

2. Character questions

You will be asked about a character from the text on the paper. You may be asked what type of person you think they are, how they relate to the other characters or how we know

something about their personality. Your answer should be based around three things:
1. What the character **does.**
2. What the character **says.**
3. How the writer **describes** the character.

In your answer you should make your point, use a quotation to support it and explain your point.

3. Atmosphere questions

You may be asked how the writer creates atmosphere or tension in the extract. Writers usually create tension by:
- Using very short sentences, e.g. 'The night was dark. No sound could be heard.'
- Using dialogue.
- Describing the atmosphere using adjectives (describing words) and similes (comparisons using the words 'like' or 'as'), e.g. 'The wind cut through him like a razor.'

Try to identify the use of any of these techniques in the extract.

4. Opinion questions

You may be asked your opinion on some aspect of the extract. In your answer, try to be positive. Saying that you don't like the piece because it is boring doesn't help the examiner to give you marks. Look at the various aspects of the extract and use them as reasons why you like it. The following list may give you some ideas:
- **Characters**: You could say that you liked the central character and how they related to the other characters. Or you could identify with the central character, especially if the writer tells us what is going on in the character's head.
- **Dialogue**: The dialogue is any written direct speech in the piece. Writers often use dialogue to make the scene seem more realistic and to create tension. You could say you liked the use of dialogue as it made the piece realistic or added tension, humour or suspense to the extract.
- **Descriptive passage:** If the writer describes the scene very well using adjectives and similes, then you could comment on this aspect of the piece. For example: 'Tom fell out of a top-floor window into a concrete mixer. It churned a couple of times, then spat him out like a cannonball.' Here the writer compares Tom to a cannonball (simile).

Read this extract adapted from *The Door* by Margrit Cruickshank, taken from the 2009 exam paper, and answer the questions that follow.

The Door

by Margaret Cruickshank

Ma wasn't in when I got home. I went into the kitchen, took three white bread rolls out of the freezer and defrosted them in the microwave. I filled one with butter and crisps, the second with ham, chutney, peanuts and salad, and the third with banana and raspberry jam: starters, main course and sweet. A man needs sustenance after a hard day at school.

Heaping the whole lot on to a plate with a glass of milk, I went into the den, switched on the television, put my feet up on the couch and watched Jerry the mouse outwit Tom the cat on children's television. Tom fell out of a top floor window into a concrete mixer. It churned a couple of times, then spat him out like a cannonball. He flew through the air, crashed against the garden fence and landed on the gatepost just as Ma's key grated in the front door.

I took my feet off the couch and tried, unsuccessfully, to hide my plate. Too late. 'Hugh! How often do I have to tell you you're not to eat in the drawing room? Why do I have to keep repeating things one million times?'

I smiled up at her. 'And it's nice to see you too, Mother dear. Yes, I did have a good day at school. And how was yours?'

'Lousy, And it has certainly not been improved by coming home and finding my one and only son dragging food all through the house and stuffing himself so full he'll leave half his dinner on his plate. You're not a baby any more, you know, that needs feeding every three hours. You're supposed to be almost a man.'

'Thanks for that "almost", Ma. I am touched.'

'You know what I mean. And, if you want to be treated like an adult, behave like one. Take that plate out into the kitchen. And pick up all the crumbs you've dropped on the carpet. Honestly, Hugh. You think I have nothing better to do than clean up after you all the time.'

I picked up most of the crumbs and stood up. 'You like it. You know you do. Makes you feel wanted.'

Ma sighed. 'Oh, get out of here. Haven't you any homework to do?'

'Nope. We're in Transition Year, remember? We had three free periods today: I got it all done in school.'

She plumped up the cushions I'd been leaning against. 'Transition Year. A waste of time, I call it. You don't seem to do any work at all.'

'Ah but we do. We have Life Skills and Media Studies and Drama and...'

She grinned. 'OK. Then practise your life skills by clearing away the mess I'm sure you've made in the kitchen and peel some potatoes for me.' She gestured at the television, where Tom was climbing up the drainpipe to get at Jerry again. 'Or is this part of your Media Studies?'

A. (i) What did Hugh do when he heard his mother coming in? (5)

(ii) How did Ma greet Hugh when she arrived home? (5)

B. From your reading of the first two paragraphs, how would you describe Hugh's character? (10)

C. Would you say that Hugh's home is a happy one?
Give reasons for your answer. (10)

D. Would you say that Ma is:
A typical mother
or
A very strict mother
or
A very cheerful and humorous mother?
Give reasons for your answer. (10)

Sample answers

A. (i) *What did Hugh do when he heard his mother coming in?* *(5)*

When Hugh heard his mother coming in he took his feet off the couch and tried to hide his plate of food.

(ii) *How did Ma greet Hugh when she arrived home?* *(5)*

When she arrived home, Hugh's Ma greeted him with a lecture about not eating in the drawing room.

B. *From your reading of the first two paragraphs, how would you describe Hugh's character?* *(10)*

I think Hugh is a very funny character. He describes the three bread rolls he has filled as his starters, main and sweet. He also tries to justify the food by saying, 'A man needs sustenance after a hard day at school.' This is funny as he then watches cartoons, which aren't very manly.

I also think Hugh is quite childish, as he gets great enjoyment from watching Tom and Jerry.

exam TIPS

Make sure you stick to the paragraphs mentioned.

C. *Would you say that Hugh's home is a happy one?*
Give reasons for your answer. *(10)*

Yes, I think that Hugh's home is a happy one because even though his mother gives out to him as soon as she walks through the door, Hugh does not take it seriously and jokes with her saying, 'And it's nice to see you too, Mother dear.'

I also think it is a happy home as Hugh's Ma makes fun of him when asking him to tidy up; 'Then practise your life skills by clearing away the mess I'm sure you've made in the kitchen.' She also makes fun of him watching the cartoons by saying, 'Or is this part of your Media Studies?'

D. *Would you say that Ma is:*
A typical mother
or
A very strict mother
or
A very cheerful and humorous mother?
Give reasons for your answer. *(10)*

I would say she is a very typical mother as she has to repeat what she says several times to Hugh, 'Why do I have to keep repeating things one million times?'

I think she is a typical mother as she knows her son very well. For example, she tells him to tidy up the mess in the kitchen even though she hasn't seen it yet because she knows what he is like, 'the mess I'm sure you've made in the kitchen.'

Practice question

Read the following extract from the 2008 paper and answer the questions that follow.

Kidnapped and taken to H.I.V.E. where he will be trained in everything villainous by Dr Nero and his staff, Otto finds himself on an island far away from his family, friends and home, and so must work with a group of other kidnapped students to break out before it's too late.

H.I.V.E (Higher Institute for Villainous Education)

Otto woke up with a dreadful headache and was shocked to find that he was in a helicopter.

'Where am I?' Otto whispered to himself. He had no idea how he came to be there.

The helicopter was preparing to land on what appeared to be the crater of an active volcano. They began to descend into the boiling black clouds and, to Otto's surprise, they weren't burnt to a cinder but continued their descent.

Suddenly, the clouds disappeared and beneath them lay a cavernous floodlit bay on which they landed.

Immediately, several dozen heavily armed men in orange jumpsuits approached the helicopter. One of them opened the door and gestured to Otto to get out. As he alighted he heard a sudden grinding noise and looked up to see two huge panels sliding together and closing off the crater entrance to the landing bay. Otto shuddered with fear. He was now totally sealed off from the outside world. 'Proceed up the stairs,' the guard ordered gruffly and, as Otto reached the top, heavy metal doors rumbled open. He entered another enormous floodlit cavern, at the centre of which was a stage.

Around this stage about twenty boys and girls stood whispering nervously together. Guards, who looked like thugs, stood around the room watching them carefully. A door hissed open and a tall, dark-haired, imposing man strode purposefully into the room. Everything about this man was impressive, from his immaculate black suit and blood-red shirt to his handsome face and his look of cool calculation.

'Welcome, ladies and gentlemen, to your new home,' he began. 'I am Dr Nero and I am the founder and controller of this Institute. Your lives, as you once knew them, are now over. You have all been carefully selected from around the world because you are unique and special. Each one of you has within you a rare talent for the supremely villainous. Here, we want to see you blossom into all that you can be, to make you the very worst that you can be. Today, all of you have the unique privilege of becoming the newest students of the world's first and only school of applied villainy. Welcome to H.I.V.E, The Higher Institute of Villainous Education!' He looked around him at the stunned boys and girls and asked with a cold smile: 'Now, are there any questions?'

Source: Adapted from *H.I.V.E.* by Mark Walden

Questions

A. In the first fifteen lines of this extract, what evidence is there that we have entered a strange world? (10)

B. Does the writer succeed in convincing you that Dr. Nero is a nasty character? Give reasons for your answer. (10)

C. Would you say that the tone of this extract is:
Frightening
or
Ridiculous
or
Amusing?
Give reasons for your answer. (10)

D. This extract is taken from the opening chapter of the novel. Would you be interested in continuing to read this book? Why/why not? (10)

Studied fiction

In the last question in the fiction section **you are asked about the novel or short story you have studied.** Each year the question varies, but essentially there are several things you need to be able to write about concerning your novel or short story.

1. Character

From your novel or short story, you need to be able to discuss one or more characters from the book. You also must be able to discuss **how they changed** in the novel and what caused that change. How did the main character relate to other characters in the book? Why did you find the main character interesting?

2. Key moments

You need to be able to identify the key moments in the novel or short story, describe them and **say why they are important.** They may be important events that change the course of the novel, or change the life of a character. You should be able to outline how the key moment had an impact on the rest of the novel.

3. Relationships

You need to be able to describe a central relationship in the novel or short story. What is the relationship like at the beginning of the story? How does it change in the middle of the story? What caused that change? At the end of the story, how are things different?

4. Beginning/end of the story

How does the story begin? Does the writer use a description of a scene or does he jump straight in with dialogue? How are the main characters introduced? At the end of the novel how is the plot resolved? Does everything end happily for all characters? You may be asked to comment on this aspect of the novel.

5. Opinion

You should have formed an opinion of the story. Try to be **positive** – focus on the good parts of the story and think about the parts of it that you particularly enjoyed. You may be asked what you thought of the story or to write a review of it, so try to be balanced in your opinion.

Preparing for the exam

At this stage you should have read and prepared a novel or short story for the exam. But, if you find you are running out of time and need to prepare for the fiction section of the exam, read the following short story and use it to prepare your answers for the exam questions that follow.

The Sniper

by Liam O'Flaherty

The long June twilight faded into night. Dublin lay enveloped in darkness but for the dim light of the moon that shone through fleecy clouds, casting a pale light as of approaching dawn over the streets and the dark waters of the Liffey. Around the beleaguered Four Courts the heavy guns roared. Here and there through the city, machine guns and rifles broke the silence of the night, spasmodically, like dogs barking on lone farms. Republicans and Free Staters were waging civil war.

On a rooftop near O'Connell Bridge, a Republican sniper lay watching. Beside him lay his rifle and over his shoulders was slung a pair of field glasses. His face was the face of a student, thin and ascetic, but his eyes had the cold gleam of the fanatic. They were deep and thoughtful, the eyes of a man who is used to looking at death.

He was eating a sandwich hungrily. He had eaten nothing since morning. He had been too excited to eat. He finished the sandwich, and, taking a flask of whiskey from his pocket, he took a short drought. Then he returned the flask to his pocket. He paused for a moment, considering whether he should risk a smoke. It was dangerous. The flash might be seen in the darkness, and there were enemies watching. He decided to take the risk.

Placing a cigarette between his lips, he struck a match, inhaled the smoke hurriedly and put out the light. Almost immediately, a bullet flattened itself against the parapet of the roof. The sniper took another whiff and put out the cigarette. Then he swore softly and crawled away to the left.

Cautiously he raised himself and peered over the parapet. There was a flash and a bullet whizzed over his head. He dropped immediately. He had seen the flash. It came from the opposite side of the street.

He rolled over the roof to a chimney stack in the rear, and slowly drew himself up behind it, until his eyes were level with the top of the parapet. There was nothing to be seen – just the dim outline of the opposite housetop against the blue sky. His enemy was under cover.

Just then an armoured car came across the bridge and advanced slowly up the street. It stopped on the opposite side of the street, fifty yards ahead. The sniper could hear the dull panting of the motor. His heart beat faster. It was an enemy car. He wanted to fire, but he knew it was useless. His bullets would never pierce the steel that covered the grey monster.

Then round the corner of a side street came an old woman, her head covered by a tattered shawl. She began to talk to the man in the turret of the car. She was pointing to the roof where the sniper lay. An informer.

The turret opened. A man's head and shoulders appeared, looking toward the sniper. The sniper raised his rifle and fired. The head fell heavily on the turret wall. The woman darted toward the side street. The sniper fired again. The woman whirled round and fell with a shriek into the gutter.

Suddenly from the opposite roof a shot rang out and the sniper dropped his rifle with a curse. The rifle clattered to the roof. The sniper thought the noise would wake the dead. He stooped to pick the rifle up. He couldn't lift it. His forearm was dead. 'I'm hit,' he muttered.

Dropping flat onto the roof, he crawled back to the parapet. With his left hand he felt the injured right forearm. The blood was oozing through the sleeve of his coat. There was no pain – just a deadened sensation, as if the arm had been cut off.

Quickly he drew his knife from his pocket, opened it on the breastwork of the parapet, and ripped open the sleeve. There was a small hole where the bullet had entered. On the other side there was no hole. The bullet had lodged in the bone. It must have fractured it. He bent the arm below the wound. The arm bent back easily. He ground his teeth to overcome the pain.

Then taking out his field dressing, he ripped open the packet with his knife. He broke the neck of the iodine bottle and let the bitter fluid drip into the wound. A paroxysm of pain swept through him. He placed the cotton wadding over the wound and wrapped the dressing over it. He tied the ends with his teeth.

Then he lay still against the parapet, and, closing his eyes, he made an effort of will to overcome the pain.

In the street beneath all was still. The armoured car had retired speedily over the bridge, with the machine gunner's head hanging lifeless over the turret. The woman's corpse lay still in the gutter.

The sniper lay still for a long time nursing his wounded arm and planning escape. Morning must not find him wounded on the roof. The enemy on the opposite roof covered his escape. He must kill that enemy and he could not use his rifle. He had only a revolver to do it. Then he thought of a plan.

Taking off his cap, he placed it over the muzzle of his rifle. Then he pushed the rifle slowly upward over the parapet, until the cap was visible from the opposite side of the street. Almost immediately there was a report, and a bullet pierced the centre of the cap. The sniper slanted the rifle forward. The cap clipped down into the street. Then catching the rifle in the middle, the sniper dropped his left hand over the roof and let it hang, lifelessly. After a few moments he let the rifle drop to the street. Then he sank to the roof, dragging his hand with him.

Crawling quickly to his feet, he peered up at the corner of the roof. His ruse had succeeded. The other sniper, seeing the cap and rifle fall, thought that he had killed his man. He was now standing before a row of chimney pots, looking across, with his head clearly silhouetted against the western sky.

The Republican sniper smiled and lifted his revolver above the edge of the parapet. The distance was about fifty yards – a hard shot in the dim light, and his right arm was paining him like a thousand devils. He took a steady aim. His hand trembled with eagerness. Pressing his lips together, he took a deep breath through his nostrils and fired. He was almost deafened with the report and his arm shook with the recoil.

Then when the smoke cleared, he peered across and uttered a cry of joy. His enemy had been hit. He was reeling over the parapet in his death agony. He struggled to keep his feet, but he was slowly falling forward as if in a dream. The rifle fell from his grasp, hit the parapet, fell over, bounded off the pole of a barber's shop beneath and then clattered on the pavement.

Then the dying man on the roof crumpled up and fell forward. The body turned over and over in space and hit the ground with a dull thud. Then it lay still.

The sniper looked at his enemy falling and he shuddered. The lust of battle died in him. He became bitten by remorse. The sweat stood out in beads on his forehead. Weakened by his wound and the long summer day of fasting and watching on the roof, he revolted from the sight of the shattered mass of his dead enemy. His teeth chattered, he began to gibber to himself, cursing the war, cursing himself, cursing everybody.

He looked at the smoking revolver in his hand, and with an oath he hurled it to the roof at his feet. The revolver went off with a concussion and the bullet whizzed past the sniper's head. He was frightened back to his senses by the shock. His nerves steadied. The cloud of fear scattered from his mind and he laughed.

Taking the whiskey flask from his pocket, he emptied it a drought. He felt reckless under the influence of the spirit. He decided to leave the roof now and look for his company commander, to report. Everywhere around was quiet. There was not much danger in going through the streets. He picked up his revolver and put it in his pocket. Then he crawled down through the skylight to the house underneath.

When the sniper reached the laneway on the street level, he felt a sudden curiosity as to the identity of the enemy sniper whom he had killed. He decided that he was a good shot, whoever he was. He wondered did he know him. Perhaps he had been in his own company before the split in the army. He decided to risk going over to have a look at him. He peered around the corner into O'Connell Street. In the upper part of the street there was heavy firing, but around here all was quiet.

The sniper darted across the street. A machine gun tore up the ground around him with a hail of bullets, but he escaped. He threw himself face downward beside the corpse. The machine gun stopped.

Then the sniper turned over the dead body and looked into his brother's face.

1. How does the writer set the scene of the story?
2. What do we learn about the character of the sniper?
3. What does he do or say that gives you this impression of him?
4. How does the rivalry between the two snipers develop?
5. What is your opinion of the end of the story?

Name a **novel** or **short story** you have studied which deals with an important relationship.

- Name the characters in the relationship.
- Describe how this relationship develops.
- Choose your favourite character in this relationship and explain why this is your favourite character. (2009) (20)

Name the novel or short story and the author in the first line of your answer.

Sample answer on a short story

The short story I have studied is 'The Sniper' by Liam O'Flaherty.

The two characters in the relationship are the Republican sniper and his brother, the Free State sniper.

At the beginning of the story we are not aware that the Free State sniper is the main character's brother. The Republican sniper is on a rooftop near O'Connell Bridge and he is spotted by another sniper from the opposite side of the street. The relationship between the two gunmen develops during the story when the Republican sniper fires at an armoured car and a woman. The other gunman fires at him and he is wounded. He then has to outwit his brother to escape from the rooftop. He thinks of a plan to confuse the other sniper by making him think he was dead. In the confusion, the Free state sniper stood up and the Republican sniper shot him dead. At the end of the story the Republican sniper goes to identify the body and discovers he has killed his own brother.

exam TIPS

Divide up your answer into the same headings as the question. It makes it easier for the examiner to give you marks!

My favourite character in this story is the Republican sniper, as he is a very strong-willed character, even when he is shot he manages to bandage his own wound and outwit his enemy. He is also very clever as he makes the other sniper think that he is dead and manages to shoot him with only one good arm. However there are a few things I didn't like about this character. He is very violent, he shoots at the armoured car and the woman on the street and in the end he kills his own brother.

Sample answer on a novel

The novel I have studied is 'Goodnight Mr Tom' by Michelle Magorian.

The two characters in the relationship are William Beech, an evacuee from London, and Mr Tom Oakley, the elderly man who takes him in.

At the beginning of the novel, the relationship between the two is very strained. Willie doesn't know how to act around Tom and is terrified by Tom's dog. Tom isn't used to being around children and doesn't know what to do with William. During the novel, however, their relationship progresses. Tom teaches Willie how to read and praises him for his achievements. Willie helps Tom to get involved in the community again by playing the organ for the choir and getting over his wife's death. By the end of the novel Tom saves Willie by rescuing him from the cupboard his mother locked him in and Tom adopts Willie.

My favourite character is Willie Beech as he really grows as a character in the novel. He learns to read and write and discovers that he can act and draw. He suffered a very hard life with his mother but by the end of the novel he has a better future ahead of him with Mr Tom. Willie also helps Mr Tom and encourages him to be part of the community again.

There is a lot more you can say about a novel rather than a short story, so if you can, make sure you have a novel prepared for the exam.

Practice questions

All questions are worth 20 marks.

1. Name a novel or short story you have studied in which something strange or unexpected happens.
   - Describe the event that happens.
   - How were people's lives affected by this event?
   - Did the author succeed in convincing you that this strange or unexpected event could really have happened? Explain why/why not. (2008)
2. Name a novel or short story you have studied in which there is an element of fantasy.
   - Describe the element of fantasy in the novel or short story.
   - Describe how the life of an individual or of a group of people is changed by the element of fantasy. (2007)

3. Name a novel or short story you have studied in which something extraordinarily good or bad happens to an individual or a group of people.
   - Describe what happened.
   - Explain what caused it to happen.
   - Describe how the life of the individual or of the group was changed by what happened. (2007)
4. Name a novel or short story you have studied in which a character undergoes a change.
   - Describe the character at the beginning of the novel or short story.
   - Explain who or what caused the character to change.
   - Describe the character at the end.
   - Did you prefer the character before or after the change had taken place? Give reasons for your answer. (2006)
5. Think about a novel or short story you have studied. A storyteller often begins by:
   - Describing a scene, a place or an incident.
   - Introducing a character or two.
   - Writing what the characters say in dialogue.

   Describe the beginning of the story you have studied.
   Was it a good beginning? Why or why not? (2002)

5 Poetry

- To understand the key concepts of poetry.
- To interpret the **unseen poetry** in the exam.
- To write a concise answer on your **studied poetry**.

Understanding poetry

Poetry is a picture in words. The poet tries to capture a moment or a memory or an event, in words. The words he or she chooses are important, as every word has meaning and is chosen for a reason. Like an artist, the poet may use certain **techniques** to describe the scene, such as imagery or comparison.

But as well as creating a **visual picture**, poetry uses another sense – **sound**. The poet knows how certain words sound and uses these sounds to create rhythm and rhyme in the poem.

In the exam you have two tasks to complete:

- You must examine the unseen poetry on the paper and respond to it, giving your own point of view.
- You must comment on the poetry you have already studied.

In the Junior Certificate exam the questions in the poetry section are based on an unseen poem as well as the poetry you have studied. The entire section is worth **60 marks**:

- 40 for your answers on the unseen poem.
- 20 for the poetry you have studied throughout the year.

As with each section of this paper, you have approximately **25 minutes** to read and answer each section.

If **poetry** is in **Section 4** of the exam then it **must** be answered. If it is in Section 5, 6 or 7 then you have the option of leaving out this section.

Unseen poetry

On the paper, you are given a poem that you may not have seen before to read and then asked to answer the questions that follow. Some students find this task terrifying and try to avoid the poetry section of the exam. The key point is to take your time and read the poem carefully.

When answering any question on poetry there are only two things you need to keep in mind:

1 What is the poet trying to say (**content** of the poem)?
2 How does the poet say it (**style** of the poem)?

- Read the **title** of the poem carefully! This could give you a sense of what the poem is about.
- Read the poem **slowly**. Make sure you understand what happens in the poem. Don't jump to conclusions.
- **Reread** the poem. Identify any words or phrases that stand out.
- Sometimes the poem is accompanied by an **illustration** that may help you to understand what the poem is about. Just be careful to base your answers on the poem and not on the picture.

Content

What the poem is about can usually be uncovered if you ask yourself a few questions while reading it.

Poetry Checklist:	
Who is speaking in the poem?	✓
What happens in the poem?	✓
When does the poem take place?	✓
Where is the poem set?	✓
How does the poet feel?	✓

If you can answer all these questions then you understand the poem enough to write a very good answer in the exam.

Always read the unseen poem several times to make sure you understand what the poet is trying to say.

Style and techniques

The **style** of a poet is the way he or she writes. You don't need to be afraid of writing about the poet's style as you will probably have picked up on some aspects of the style when you first read the poem, but you just didn't know how to explain it.

Poets use certain **techniques** in their poetry. It is up to you to identify these techniques and comment on them in your answers. If you can identify these techniques in the unseen poem and comment on them in your answer, you are showing the examiner that you understand poetry! Here are some common techniques used by poets, as well as some aspects of style, that you may encounter in the unseen poem. Remember, you can also look at the poetry you have studied and prepared for the exam under these headings.

Feelings, mood and atmosphere

The poet's feelings or the mood of the poem are often shown or conveyed by the words that the poet chooses. No word in a poem is just there by chance. The poet has taken his/her time and chosen the words that **best describe** the feeling he/she wanted to **convey** or show. It is up to you to look at the words in the poem and decide what the poet was trying to convey.

The word **convey** is often used on the exam paper, it simply means 'to show'.

The words chosen by the poet tell us the mood of the poem. Is the poem optimistic or pessimistic? Does the poet use dark, depressing imagery or bright, joyful words and phrases?

Look at the following lines and assess the feelings and mood of the poet.

> 'Around the/Gable-end a starved wind razors and from/The split gutters icicles hang like fangs.'
> ('Visitor' by Wes Magee)

> 'When all at once I saw a crowd,/a host of golden daffodils;/Beside the lake beneath the trees,/fluttering and dancing in the breeze.'
> ('I wandered lonely as a cloud' by William Wordsworth)

Both poems describe the wind, but the words chosen by each poet create a very different atmosphere or mood in the poem.

In the first poem the poet uses words like *starved*, *razors* and *fangs*. All of these words are very **negative** and make the wind seem very harsh and cruel. In the second poem the poet uses words that are **gentle and positive** such as *fluttering* and *dancing*. This creates a very calm, peaceful atmosphere.

You can comment on the mood or atmosphere created by the poet in your answer in the exam – just make sure you can **support the point you make by quoting a word or phrase** from the poem.

You could say: 'In this poem the poet creates a very cruel and negative atmosphere by using the words "starved", "razors" and "fangs" to describe the wind.'

Techniques

Alliteration: Words that begin with the same letter

Examples: **Kn**ock-**kn**eed,
Forest's **f**erny **f**loor,
Grab and **gr**apple

The poet uses alliteration to add **emphasis** to the poem, to draw the reader's attention to a certain point or to create certain sounds in the poem. Some letters create very soft sounds and so have a calming effect, while others are quite harsh and create a negative, grating sound.

Repeatedly using the letter 's' has a special name, **sibilance.** Sibilance is used regularly in poetry to create a soft, gentle sound, e.g. 'Snowdrops and candles soothed the bedside', 'Silence surged softly'.

Assonance: Words that use the same vowel sounds

Examples: M**oo**nlit d**oo**r
Cl**i**pped s**i**des

The poet uses assonance to speed up or slow down the line. In general, broad vowels (a, o, u) tend to slow down the line and make the line seem more sad, e.g. 'f**o**re bem**o**aned m**o**an', but the slender vowels (i, e) tend to quicken the line and make the poem seem more lively.

Simile: A comparison using the words 'like' or 'as'

Examples: His face was **as** white **as** snow.
The playground emptied just **as** though a plug was pulled.

The poet uses similes to expand on the images created in the poem. This helps us to imagine exactly what the poet wants us to see.

Metaphor: A comparison not using the words 'like' or 'as'

Examples: Our yells were wolves howling.
The sea is a hungry dog.

The poet uses metaphors to make the comparison more dramatic.

Repetition: Repeating a word or phrase.

Examples: 'A scrap! A scrap!'
'Looking for you and me, my dear, looking for you and me.'

The poet uses repetition to make a moment more dramatic or urgent or sad.

Other aspects of poetry that you should be able to comment on are:

- **Imagery:** The words or phrases that create pictures in your head.
- **Rhyme**: The words that rhyme in the poem. They may be close together and regular or far apart and irregular. Look at what effect this has on the poem.
- **Rhythm:** This is the rhythm or beat created by the sounds of the words as they are said aloud. The rhythm may change in a poem and it usually reflects the mood, that is, a quick lively rhythm reflects a bright happy mood.
- **Language:** Look at the types of words used by the poet. Does the poet use unusual words? Are slang words used or does the poet stick to very formal language?

Don't worry about this long list. If you can identify one or two aspects of style in a poem then you are doing very well!

Exam questions on the unseen poem

The following are the types of questions you may be asked in the unseen poetry section of the paper:

- Where does the poem take place?
- Why does the poet make this comparison?
- What were the reactions of the people in the poem?
- Name two things the poet notices.
- What is your favourite word or image from the poem?
- What sort of person is the poet?
- Give two reasons why you think this poem deserved a prize.
- Who is speaking in the poem?
- How does the person in the poem feel?
- What happens in the poem?
- At what time of year do you think this takes place?
- Why do you think the poet uses this title for the poem?
- What kind of relationship do the characters have in the poem?
- What message or lesson do you take from the poem?

In the exam, the first three or four questions are based on the poem printed on the paper. These questions are worth 40 marks in total.

The last question relates to the poetry you have studied. This question is worth 20 marks.

How to answer the exam question:

- Read the question carefully. **Underline** the **key words** in the question.
- Make sure you use **full sentences**.
- Use the key words from the question in your answer.
- Use **quotes** from the poem on the paper to prove your point.
- Don't misspell words that are printed on the paper!
- Write according to the marks allowed, e.g. a 10-mark question requires eight to ten lines in your answer, but a 5-mark question requires just one or two sentences.
- To make sure you don't throw away marks, make sure you answer **all** the questions in each section. Every year some students leave out the 20-mark question and lose valuable marks!

Make sure you answer the questions according to the marks awarded for them. In other words, you should spend twice as much time on a 20-mark question as you have spent on a 10-mark question.

Read this poem from the 2009 exam paper and answer the questions that follow.

One Question from a Bullet

by John Agard
(Adapted for the 2009 exam paper)

I want to give up being a bullet
I've been a bullet too long

I want to be an innocent coin
in the hand of a child
and be squeezed through the slot
of a bubblegum machine

I want to give up being a bullet
I've been a bullet too long

I want to be a good luck seed
lying idle in somebody's pocket
or some ordinary little stone
on the way to becoming an earring
or just lying there unknown
among a crowd of other ordinary stones.

I want to give up being a bullet
I've been a bullet too long

The question is
Can you give up being a killer?

A. (i) Who is the speaker in this poem? (5)
(ii) Who is the speaker talking to? (5)

B. 'The Bullet doesn't want to be a bullet anymore.' Name two things it wants to be and from your reading of the poem explain why the bullet wants to be these things. (10)

C. What message or lesson do you take from the poem? Give reasons for your answer. (10)

D. What is the question the bullet asks and why do you think it asks this question? (10)

Sample answers

A. (i) *Who is the speaker in this poem?* *(5)*

The speaker in this poem is a bullet, as the opening line tells us 'I want to give up being a bullet.'

(ii) *Who is the speaker talking to?* *(5)*

The speaker is talking to the gunman, as it says 'Can you give up being a killer?'

B. *'The Bullet doesn't want to be a bullet anymore.' Name two things it wants to be and from your reading of the poem explain why the bullet wants to be these things.* *(10)*

The speaker wants to be 'an innocent coin' or 'some ordinary stone'. I think the bullet wants to be a coin in the hand of a child as it would be an innocent life. The bullet obviously feels that being a bullet is not innocent. He wants to be an ordinary stone on the way to being an earring as this is also a positive image, and, unlike a bullet, it won't have negative consequences.

exam TIPS

- Divide up your answers the same way the questions are divided up. This gives the examiner a chance to give you marks for each section. If you stick all your answers together it is harder for them to give you marks.
- Always label the answer clearly.
- Always use full sentences!

Make sure you name **two** things and give an explanation.

C. *What message or lesson do you take from the poem? Give reasons for your answer.* *(10)*

The message I take from this poem is that the bullet is tired of its life, 'I've been a bullet too long'. The bullet wishes to be anything else but a bullet, but particularly innocent things, such as a stone or a coin. The images the poet uses of the child pushing the coin into the vending machine ('be squeezed through the slot of a bubblegum machine') suggests that this would be difficult for the bullet but he would still prefer it to his life as a bullet.

D. *What is the question the bullet asks and why do you think it asks this question?* *(10)*

The bullet asks: 'Can you give up being a killer?' I think the bullet asks this question because it has not chosen its life as a bullet. The bullet is not guilty of killing people – those who shoot the guns are the guilty ones. The bullet asks this question to make us think about our decisions and actions and what consequences they may have.

Practice questions

My Gramp

by Derek Stuart

My gramp has got a medal.
On the front there is a runner.
On the back it says:
Senior Boys 100 yards
First William Green

I asked him about it,
but before he could reply
Gran said, 'Don't listen to his tales,
The only running he ever did
was after the girls.'

Gramp gave a chuckle
and went out the back
to get the tea.

As he shuffled down the passage
with his back bent,
I tried to imagine him,
legs flying, chest out,
breasting the tape.

But I couldn't.

A. What kind of medal has the poet's Gramp got? (10)

B. What are your favourite words or images from the poem? Explain why they are your favourite. (10)

C. From your reading of the poem, what kind of relationship did the poet's Gran and Gramp have? (10)

D. The last line of the poem is: 'But I couldn't.'
What couldn't the poet imagine and why couldn't he imagine it? (10)
(2008 exam paper)

Pachy, the Dinosaur
by Richard Armour

Among the later dinosaurs
Though not the largest, strongest,
PACHYCEPHALOSAURUS had
The name that was the longest.

Yet he had more than syllables,
As you may well suppose.
He had great knobs upon his cheeks
And spikes upon his nose.

Ten inches thick, atop his head,
A bump of bone projected.
By this his brain, though hardly worth
Protecting, was protected.

No claw or tooth, no tree that fell
Upon his head *kerwhacky*,
Could crack or crease or jar or scar
That stony part of Pachy.

And so he nibbled plants in peace
And lived untroubled days.
Sometimes, in fact, as Pachy proved,
To be a bonehead pays.

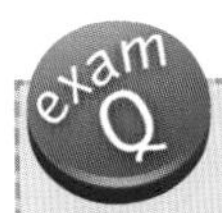

A. Referring to the poem, write a description of the dinosaur, Pachy. (10)

B. (i) What words or lines in the poem tell us that Pachy was not very brainy? (5)

(ii) Was Pachy violent? Base your answer on the poem. (5)

C. Write five pairs of rhyming words from this poem. (10)

D. What is your favourite stanza in this poem? Give reasons for your answer. (10)

(2007 exam paper)

Stanza means verse of the poem

Studied poetry

To prepare for this section of the paper, you should make sure that you have an adequate selection of poetry to answer the questions asked.

You are asked to choose a poem that you have studied that matches a heading given. You are generally asked to:

- Name the poem and poet.
- Describe what happens in the poem.
- Outline your reasons for liking/disliking the poem.
- Comment on some aspect of the poem.

Typical headings given are:

- A poem that describes a person, place or event.
- Any poem that deserved a prize.
- A poem that made you sad or angry.
- A poem that created a clear picture in your head.
- A poem that described animals, nature, weather, etc.
- A poem that made you feel happiness or joy.
- A poem that describes a memory.
- A poem that is amusing or contains vivid descriptions.
- A poem that describes home or family or friends.

To prepare for the exam, you should be able to write **three paragraphs** on your studied poems, outlining what happens in the poem, your reasons for liking/disliking the poem and a comment on some aspect of the poem, e.g. how it made you feel.

Sample poetry

The following is a selection of poetry you may use for your studied poetry section. To prepare for your exam, you should be able to answer the questions that follow each poem.

KEY THEMES: CHILDHOOD, MEMORIES, DEATH, SADNESS, EVENT

Mid-term Break

by Seamus Heaney

I sat all morning in the college sick bay
Counting bells knelling classes to a close.
At two o'clock our neighbours drove me home.

In the porch I met my father crying –
He had always taken funerals in his stride –
And Big Jim Evans saying it was a hard blow.

The baby cooed and laughed and rocked the pram
When I came in, and I was embarrassed
By old men standing up to shake my hand

And tell me they were 'sorry for my trouble',
Whispers informed strangers I was the eldest,
Away at school, as my mother held my hand

In hers and coughed out angry tearless sighs.
At ten o'clock the ambulance arrived
With the corpse, stanched and bandaged by the nurses.

Next morning I went up into the room. Snowdrops
And candles soothed the bedside; I saw him
For the first time in six weeks. Paler now,

Wearing a poppy bruise on his left temple,
He lay in the four foot box as in his cot.
No gaudy scars, the bumper knocked him clear.

A four foot box, a foot for every year.

1. Describe what happens in the poem.
2. How does the poet feel in the poem?
3. How does the poet create the vivid scene in the poem?
4. What words or phrases in the poem stand out? Why?
5. Pick out examples of:
   - Alliteration.
   - Repetition.
   - Assonance.
   - Simile.

KEY THEMES: NATURE, YOUTH, MEMORIES, GROWING UP, EVENT

The Early Purges

by Seamus Heaney

I was six when I first saw kittens drown
Dan Taggart pitched them, 'the scraggy wee shits',
Into a bucket; a frail metal sound,

Soft paws scraping like mad. But their tiny din
Was soon soused. They were slung on the snout
Of the pump and the water pumped in.

'Sure isn't it better for them now?' Dan said.
Like wet gloves they bobbed and shone till he sluiced
Them out on the dunghill, glossy and dead.

Suddenly frightened, for days I sadly hung
Round the yard, watching the three sogged remains
Turn mealy and crisp as old summer dung

Until I forgot them. But the fear came back
When Dan trapped big rats, snared rabbits, shot crows
Or, with a sickening tug, pulled old hens' necks,

Still, living displaces false sentiments
And now, when shrill pups are prodded to drown
I just shrug. 'Bloody pups'. It makes sense:

'Prevention of cruelty' talk cuts ice in town
Where they consider death unnatural —
But on well-run farms pests have to be kept down.

1. Describe what happens in the poem.
2. How do you feel having read the poem?
3. What words or phrases in the poem stand out? Why?
4. What does the poet say about nature?
5. How is this poem similar to, or different from, the previous poem by Seamus Heaney?

KEY THEMES: WAR, DEATH, ANGER, EVENT (APPLIES TO BOTH POEMS)

The General

by Siegfried Sassoon

'Good-morning; good-morning!' the General said
When we met him last week on our way to the line.
Now the soldiers he smiled at are most of 'em dead,
And we're cursing his staff for incompetent swine.
'He's a cheery old card,' grunted Harry to Jack
As they slogged up to Arras with rifle and pack.

But he did for them both by his plan of attack.

1. What happens in the poem?
2. What hardships do the soldiers face?
3. What, do you think, is the poet's opinion of the General?
4. What message does the poem have about war?

Base Details

by Siegfried Sassoon

If I were fierce, and bald, and short of breath,
I'd live with scarlet Majors at the Base,
And speed glum heroes up the line to death.
You'd see me with my puffy petulant face,
Guzzling and gulping in the best hotel,
Reading the Roll of Honour. 'Poor young chap,'
I'd say – 'I used to know his father well;
Yes we've lost heavily in that last scrap.'
And when the war is done and youth stone dead,
I'd toddle safely home and die – in bed.

1. What kind of Major does the poet describe in the poem?
2. What, do you think, is the poet's opinion of this type of Major?
3. Pick out words or phrases in the poem that you feel accurately describe the Major.
4. Can you identify the techniques used by Sassoon in this poem?
5. How is this poem different from, or similar to, the previous poem by Siegfried Sassoon?

KEY THEMES: NATURE, HAPPINESS, EVENT

I Wandered Lonely as a Cloud

by William Wordsworth

I wandered lonely as a cloud
That floats on high o'er vales and hills,
When all at once I saw a crowd,
A host of golden daffodils;
Beside the lake, beneath the trees,
Fluttering and dancing in the breeze.

Continuous as the stars that shine
And twinkle on the Milky Way,
They stretched in never-ending line
Along the margin of a bay:
Ten thousand saw I at a glance,
Tossing their heads in sprightly dance.

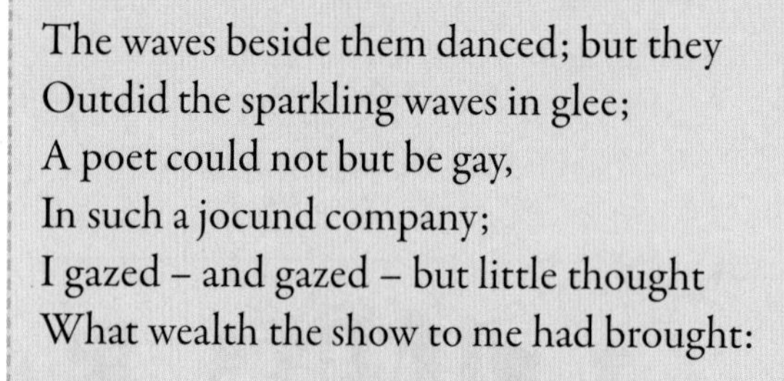

The waves beside them danced; but they
Outdid the sparkling waves in glee;
A poet could not but be gay,
In such a jocund company;
I gazed – and gazed – but little thought
What wealth the show to me had brought:

For oft, when on my couch I lie
In vacant or in pensive mood,
They flash upon that inward eye
Which is the bliss of solitude;
And then my heart with pleasure fills,
And dances with the daffodils.

1. Describe what happens in the poem.
2. What words in the poem show the happiness of the poet?
3. What words or images from the poem stand out? Why?
4. What is the poet's attitude towards nature?

KEY THEMES: MYSTERY, EVENT, DESCRIBING A SCENE

The Listeners

by Walter de la Mare

'Is there anybody there?' said the Traveller,
Knocking on the moonlit door;
And his horse in the silence champed the grasses
Of the forest's ferny floor:
And a bird flew up out of the turret,
Above the Traveller's head:
And he smote upon the door again a second time;
'Is there anybody there?' he said.
But no one descended to the Traveller;
No head from the leaf-fringed sill
Leaned over and looked into his grey eyes,
Where he stood perplexed and still.
But only a host of phantom listeners
That dwelt in the lone house then
Stood listening in the quiet of the moonlight
To that voice from the world of men:
Stood thronging the faint moonbeams on the dark stair,
That goes down to the empty hall,
Hearkening in an air stirred and shaken
By the lonely Traveller's call.
And he felt in his heart their strangeness,
Their stillness answering his cry,
While his horse moved, cropping the dark turf,
'Neath the starred and leafy sky;
For he suddenly smote on the door, even
Louder, and lifted his head: –
'Tell them I came, and no one answered,
That I kept my word,' he said.
Never the least stir made the listeners,
Though every word he spake
Fell echoing through the shadowiness of the still house
From the one man left awake:
Ay, they heard his foot upon the stirrup,
And the sound of iron on stone,
And how the silence surged softly backward,
When the plunging hoofs were gone.

1. Describe what happens in the poem.
2. How does the poet create a sense of mystery?
3. The poet uses a lot of sibilance (repeated use of 's' sound). What effect does this have on the poem?
4. What words does the poet use that show that this poem was written a long time ago?

KEY THEMES: CHILDHOOD, SCHOOL, CONFLICT

Fight!

by Barrie Wade

'A scrap! A scrap!'
The tingle in the scalp
starts us running.

The shout drains
our playground just as though
a plug was pulled

here in the space
in which two twisted, furious
bodies writhe.

Rules will not prise
these savages apart.
No ref will interpose

with shouts of 'Break!'
This contest has one single
vicious round

of grab and grapple,
wrestle, thump and scrabble,
flail and scratch.

We take no sides.
Our yells are wolves howling
for blood of any kind.

Our fingers clench.
The thrill claws our throats
like raging thirst.

The whistle shrills
and splits our pack. The circle
heaves and shatters.

The fighters still
are blind and deaf, won't hear
or see until,

parted, they go limp
as cubs drawn by the scruff
from some hot lair.

Now they are tame,
Standing outside Sir's room
grinning their shame.

Chastened, we feel
the snarls of wildness
stifle in us.

1. What happens in the poem?
2. How does the poet make the boys sound like animals?
3. How does the crowd react?
4. Pick an image you like from the poem and explain why you like it.
5. The poet uses many similes and metaphors. Give examples from the poem.

KEY THEMES: LOVE, LOSS, MEMORIES

In My Life

by Lennon and McCartney

There are places I'll remember
All my life though some have changed
Some forever not for better
Some have gone and some remain

All these places have their moments
With lovers and friends
I still can recall
Some are dead and some are living
In my life I've loved them all

But of all these friends and lovers
There is no one compares with you
And these memories lose their meaning
When I think of love as something new

Though I know I'll never lose affection
For people and things that went before
I know I'll often stop
And think about them
In my life I love you more

Though I know I'll never lose affection
For people and things that went before
I know I'll often stop
And think about them
In my life I love you more
In my life I love you more

1. What does the poet feel in this poem/lyric?
2. How does he show his feelings?
3. Pick a line from the poem that you like and explain why.

KEY THEMES: DESCRIBING A PERSON, CHILDHOOD, MEMORY

Tich Miller

By Wendy Cope

Tich Miller wore glasses
with elastoplast-pink frames
and had one foot three sizes larger than the other.

When they picked teams for outdoor games
she and I were always the last two
left standing by the wire mesh fence.

We avoided one another's eyes,
stooping, perhaps, to re-tie a shoelace,
or affecting interest in the flight

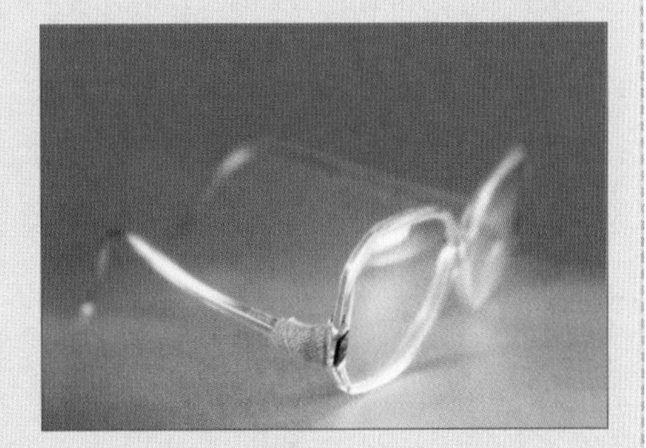

of some unfortunate bird, and pretended
not to hear the urgent conference:
'Have Tubby!' 'No, no, have Tich!'

Usually they chose me, the lesser dud,
and she lolloped, unselected
to the back of the other team.

At eleven we went to different schools.
In time I learned to get my own back,
sneering at hockey-players who couldn't spell.

Tich died when she was twelve.

1. Describe Tich Miller.
2. What happens in the poem?
3. How does the poem make you feel?

- When answering the last question in the poetry section you may use some of the poetry in this section or other poetry you have studied during the year.
- Your first sentence should name the poem and poet you are focusing on.
- Know how to spell the names of the poems and poets!
- State clearly what theme you are talking about.
- Use quotations from the poems to support your points. This means you need to learn quotes from each poem.
- Quotes don't have to be long – they may be just a word!
- Make sure you know what happens in each poem and some elements of style for each poem.
- Divide your answer into paragraphs; use the divisions in the question.
- Be able to sum up the poem in a paragraph.
- Be able to give reasons as to why you like the poem.
- It is easier to be **positive** in your answer. Saying you don't like the poem leaves you with nothing to say. Your aim is to pick up marks, not throw them away!

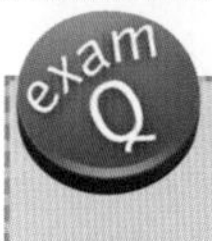

Choose a poem you have studied which describes a place or a person or an event.

- Name the poem and the poet.
- Describe what the poem is about.
- Say why you liked or disliked the poem you have chosen. (20)

(2009)

Sample answer

The poem that I have studied that describes an event is 'Fight!' by Barrie Wade.

The poem describes a fight in a playground. The poem starts with someone shouting 'A scrap! A scrap!' and everyone in the playground gathers around the fight. The fight is very vicious and the poet describes the two fighters as 'savages'. Then a whistle sounds and the crowd breaks apart. The two fighters still fight until they are pulled apart. At the end of the poem they are standing outside the teacher's door feeling ashamed but grinning.

I liked this poem because it is very descriptive. The poet uses a simile to describe the way the crowd moves in the playground, 'The shout drains the playground just as though a plug was pulled.' He also describes the savagery of the fighters and the crowd by using many animal images throughout the poem, such as, 'our yells are wolves howling' and 'they go limp as cubs'. I also thought it was a very realistic description of a playground fight. He makes it seem more realistic when he uses words like 'A scrap!'

Practice questions

1. Choose any poem you have studied which you feel deserves a prize.
   - Name the poem and the poet.
   - Describe what the poem is about.
   - Say why you think it deserves a prize. (20)

   (2004)

2. Name a poem you have studied which made you feel sad **OR** angry.
   - What was the poem about?
   - Explain how the poet made you feel this sadness or this anger. (20)

   (2003)

3. Think about poems you have studied.
   Choose a poem that left *a clear picture* in your mind.
   - Name the poem and the poet.
   - Describe the picture it left in your mind.
   - Did you like or dislike the poem?
   - Say why you liked or disliked the poem. (20)

   (2002)

4. Think about poems you have studied and choose one which is amusing **OR** contains vivid descriptions.
   - Name the poem and the poet.
   - Describe how the poet succeeds in making the poem you have chosen either amusing or vivid. (20)

   (2007)

5. Think about poems you have studied and choose one which best describes a young person who is *either* happy *or* sad.
   - Name the poem and the poet. (5)
   - Describe the sad picture or the happy picture of the young person in the poem. (5)
   - How does the poet give the impression of sadness or happiness? (5)
   - Say why you liked or disliked the poem you have chosen. (5)

   (2006)

6 Drama

- To understand the **unseen drama** extract on the paper.
- To write focused answers on the **studied drama** section.

This section is worth **60 marks**. If this appears in Section 4, it is compulsory. If it appears in Section 5, 6 or 7 then you have a choice to answer two of the three sections on the paper.

Some students are fearful of trying to answer the drama section on the paper as it seems quite difficult. In fact, nothing could be further from the truth. Think of drama as a film script. Try to imagine actors saying their lines, and imagine the setting around them and you should be well able to answer the questions on the paper.

- This section begins with a piece of unseen drama that you must read. **Questions A, B, C** and **D** are usually based on this extract.
- These questions are usually worth **10 marks each**. Your answers should be approximately 10 lines for each question and should include relevant quotations from the extract where necessary.
- **Question E** usually relates to the **play or film** you have studied and is worth **20 marks**. You should be able to write two or three paragraphs on the play or film you have studied.

Unseen drama

The extract on the paper is usually taken from a play, but may be a section from a film script. You will be given background information to tell you what happened before this scene.

- Read the **introduction** to the extract carefully, as it will give you information about the background to the piece and will probably explain who each of the characters are.
- Read the extract at least twice to make sure you fully understand what is taking place. Make sure you are aware of the **key characters** and their relationship to each other. What do they do or say in the extract that reveals their attitude towards each other?
- Take careful note of all the **stage directions**. These are usually in italics or in brackets and they tell you what the actors are doing at this time or how they say the lines.
- Take note of the description of the scene, as this will give you an idea of when and where the scene is **set**.

Types of unseen drama questions

In the unseen drama section, there are certain types of questions you may be asked.

Comprehension questions

These types of questions test how well you understand the passage. You may be asked what happened in the piece or what one character said or did. These questions are very straightforward. Answer them clearly and to the point and you can quote from the extract to support your point. Make sure you use full sentences, for example:

Question: Where does this scene take place?
Answer: This scene takes place in an office.

Character questions

You may be asked about a character from the text and what type of person they are, or you may be asked to choose a character you would like to play from the extract. A character's personality is revealed through everything they **say** and everything they **do.** Look at the lines that the character says – what do they tell you about the type of person he/she is? Also look at the stage directions as they will tell you what the character does and can quite often tell you a lot more about the character. For example:

Question: What does this scene tell us about Joe's character?
Answer: This scene tells us that Joe is very serious, as he wants to study.

Tone of voice questions

You may be asked what tone of voice a character uses to say a particular line. In answering this question, look carefully at the **stage directions**, as they may already have indicated how the line should be said. Also look at what is happening in the scene at that time – if the characters are having an argument, for instance, it is likely that any line would be delivered in an angry tone of voice. Try not to use the same words in your answer; there are more **descriptive** words than good, bad, happy or sad.

Try to use descriptive words, such as: excited, enthusiastic, frightened, scared, aggressive, coaxing, boasting, superior, hostile, forceful, assertive, insistent, nervous, timid, terrified, cheerful, delighted, miserable, depressing, gloomy, calm, outraged, annoyed, etc.

Dialogue questions

You may be asked to write the dialogue for the **scene after** the one given or for the one **before**. The dialogue need not be longer than ten lines, so don't get caught up in your own story and write pages. Remember, you have only 25 minutes to do the whole drama section.

When writing dialogue, make sure you use the **correct dialogue layout** (the same as the dialogue on the paper) and use whatever information about the characters is given in the extract. Include your own stage directions if you wish, using a different coloured pen or putting them in brackets. Look at the extract on p. 77 to see an example of dialogue.

Atmosphere questions

You may be asked about how the writer creates a certain atmosphere in the piece, for example: how he or she creates a sense of tension. To answer this question, look at what the characters do and say. The stage directions will give you an idea of what the audience would see and the lines the characters say should give you a sense of what the atmosphere is like.

Stagecraft questions

You will be asked about things that are very specific to drama: set, costumes, props and direction. You may be asked to name the props needed in a scene, how you would describe the set needed or how you would direct a scene.

The set

The set is whatever is on stage to tell the audience **where** the action is taking place. There may be a backdrop of a painted scene to give an illusion of depth to the stage, or aspects of the scene may be painted onto flats (wooden cut-outs) at the side of the stage, or in some cases full replicas of rooms may be used on stage. So the set can refer to the physical items on stage that give you a sense of place and you can include furniture, park benches, lamp posts, etc. Look at the example of a stage set and identify the things on stage that tell you when and where the play is set.

Costumes

These are the clothes worn by the actor to give you a sense of character. We all make assumptions about people from the way they are dressed, so if you are asked to design the costume for a particular character, think about the image you want to portray. Are they old or young? Rich or poor? Scruffy or well dressed? Think not only about the clothes, but also the shoes and hairstyles of the characters, as they all give the audience their impression of the character. Look at the photograph of a character in costume. What type of person do you think they are? What gives you that impression of them?

Props

This is short for '**properties**' and means anything else handled by the actors on the stage, such as telephones, guns, pens, books, cups, a shovel, etc. They may be listed in the stage directions if they are vital to the story. Look at the photograph of a scene from a play. What items are the actors handling? These are the props.

Direction

You may be asked how you would direct a scene if you were the director. The director has complete control on the stage and it is his or her job to tell the actors where to move on stage and how to say their lines. As you read the piece, think about how you imagine it in your head. The director's job is to turn it into a reality by telling everyone else exactly what he or she wants them to do. When answering this type of question, you should focus on how you want the actor to say the lines and how you want them to move. For example, you could say, 'I would have the actor show he is angry in this scene by raising his voice at the end and by moving around the stage in quick sudden movements.'

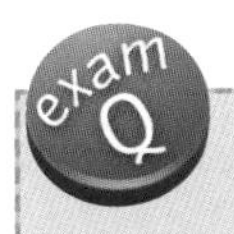

Read the following extract, a scene adapted from Brian Friel's play, *Lovers*, taken from the 2005 exam, and examine the sample answers that follow.

Joe Brennan, aged seventeen and a half, and Mag Enright, aged seventeen, are sitting on a hilltop on a beautiful June morning. They have gone up there to study for their Leaving Certificate, which will begin in a few days. Joe and Mag are going to be married in three weeks' time.

Mag: I love the view of Ballymore from up here – the town, the lake, even the people. But when I'm down among them, I can't stand them. I bet that's how God feels at times too. Wouldn't you think so?

Joe: *(Trying to study)* I don't know how God feels.

Mag: Why not?

Joe: Because I'm not God.

Mag: Oh! You're so clever.

Joe: Look Mag, we came up here to study. What are you going to do first?

Mag: French. And then Maths and then Irish. And then English language and literature. After lunch Geography and History of the World. I have a planned programme for myself. What are you starting with?
Joe: Maths.
Mag: Then what?
Joe: That's all.
Mag: Only Maths?
Joe: Huh-huh.
Mag: Then, that's what I'll do too. *(Really worried)* My God, if the volume of a cone doesn't come up, I'm scootrified! Joe... *(Pause. There is silence for few seconds)*
Joe: What?
Mag: What's the difference between language and literature?
Joe: Stupid!
Mag: What?
Joe: (*Flings his book from him in annoyance)* You-are-a bloody-pain-in-the-neck. You haven't shut up for a minute since we got here! You have done no work yourself and you have wasted my morning too! So, will you shut up!
Mag: *(With dignity)* I will. I certainly will. *(Brief pause)*. But before I go silent for the rest of the day, there's something I want to get clear between us, Joe Brennan. *(Pause)* Joe, you never proposed to me.
Joe: Huh?
Mag: You haven't asked me to marry you. Our children will want toknow. Especially the girls.
Joe: What are you raving about?
Mag: Propose to me!
Joe: God!
Mag: Now!
Joe: You really are...
Mag: Ask me!
Joe: Will-you-marry-me. Now!
Mag: Thank you, Joseph. I will.
Joe: Crazy! Absolutely, totally crazy!

A. In the last line, Joe tells Mag that she is 'Crazy! Absolutely, totally crazy!' Do you agree? Give reasons for your answer. (10)
B. How would you describe Joe's character? What does he say and do in this scene that leads you to this opinion of him? (10)
C. In what tone of voice do you think Joe speaks to Mag in this scene: annoyed? mocking? loving? amused? Give reasons for your choice. (10)
D. Imagine the scene where Mag announces to her parents that she and Joe are going to get married. Write the dialogue (about 10 lines) you think would have taken place between Mag and her parents. (10)

Sample answers

A. *In the last line, Joe tells Mag that she is 'Crazy! Absolutely, totally crazy!' Do you agree? Give reasons for your answer.* *(10)*

Yes I agree that Mag in this extract seems to be crazy. Firstly, she lists off all the subjects she is going to study but she changes her mind instantly when she hears that Joe is doing only Maths. 'Then that's what I'll do too.' She then keeps asking him silly questions and eventually wants him to propose to her because their 'children will want to know'. This seems very crazy behaviour, so I agree with Joe that Mag is totally crazy.

exam TIPS

State what your answer is, then support it with quotes from the **extract**.

B. *How would you describe Joe's character? What does he say and do in this scene that leads you to this opinion of him?* *(10)*

I think Joe is a very serious character in this extract. All he wants to do is study his maths and Mag keeps annoying him: 'Look Mag, we came up here to study.' I also think he is not very patient and is very easily annoyed. He calls Mag 'a bloody-pain-in-the-neck' when she asks him a question about language and literature. But I think he really does like Mag, as he does ask her to marry him when she keeps asking him to. 'Will-you-marry-me.'

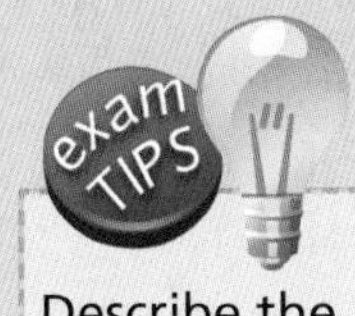

Describe the character, and support your points with quotes from the extract.

C. *In what tone of voice do you think Joe speaks to Mag in this scene: annoyed? mocking? loving? amused? Give reasons for your choice.* *(10)*

I think Joe speaks to Mag in a very **annoyed** tone of voice. From the beginning, he is trying to study and she keeps interrupting him so all his lines are very short. 'That's all.' I also think Joe speaks in an annoyed tone because the stage directions tell us that he 'flings his book from him in annoyance'. Also, the writer uses hyphens between the words to show that they are said in a very annoyed or staccato tone, 'You-are-a bloody-pain-in-the-neck'.

D. *Imagine the scene where Mag announces to her parents that she and Joe are going to get married. Write the dialogue (about 10 lines) you think would have taken place between Mag and her parents.* *(10)*

Mag: Mam, Dad, I've got something to tell you.
Mam: What, love?
Mag: I think you should sit down.
Dad: Why? What is it? What's wrong?
Mag: Nothing's wrong, Dad! It's the best news in the world! Joe and I are going to get married!
Dad: What?
Mam: What do you mean? You're too young to get married!
Mag: But we're in love, Mam!
Dad: I don't care what you think you are! You are too young to get married and that's the end of it!
Mag: You can't stop us!! We love each other and we are going to get married! *(She storms out the door)*

exam TIPS

Use the same layout as the dialogue on the paper.

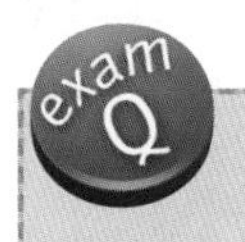

Read this scene adapted from *Just the Job* by Ann Farquhar-Smith and answer the questions which follow.

Jason O'Reilly has an appointment for an interview with the Personnel Manager at Jackson's. Before the interview, there is a discussion at home with his family.

Jason: Mom! I've got an appointment for an interview with the Personnel Manager at Jackson's on Tuesday.
Mrs O'Reilly: Well done, Jason. An interview means you've nearly got the job.
Mr O'Reilly: But he hasn't yet, has he?
Mrs O'Reilly: Appearance is most important at an interview, Jason. You'd better think about what you're going to wear.
Mr O'Reilly: Your Mother's right. You'll need to wear a suit.
Jason: But I haven't got a suit.
Mrs O'Reilly: Yes, you have. There's the one you wore to your Aunt Kate's wedding.
Jason: That won't fit me. I've grown a bit since then.
Mrs O'Reilly: I can let it out. You've not grown that much.
Julie: (Jason's sister) And you'll have to get your hair cut, and get rid of that ear-ring.

Jason:	Why? I'm not joining the army. I want a job as a fitter.
Mrs O'Reilly:	Your sister is right Jason. You've let your hair get out of hand since
you left	school and that ear-ring does nothing for your image.
Jason:	What image? I like my hair like this and ear-rings are the fashion.
Mr O'Reilly:	You may like your hair and that filthy looking stud but the Personnel Manager won't.
Jason:	I'd rather draw the dole than have a short back and sides.
Mr O'Reilly:	You can let it grow again after the interview.
Jason:	I'm not applying to be Managing Director, you know, Dad! Have I got to go to all this trouble?
Julie:	Why can't you make an effort to do the right thing for once?
Mr O'Reilly:	With jobs as scarce as they are nowadays nothing should be too much trouble.
Jason:	And nothing is what I'd like to do!

Questions

A. What advice is Jason getting at home about his interview? (10)

B. From what you read in this piece, would you give the job to Jason? Explain your answer. (10)

C. Imagine that you are the costume designer for this play. Describe the costume you would design for **ONE** of the following characters:

- Mr O' Reilly
- Mrs O' Reilly
- Julie.

Say why you have chosen your design. (10)

D. Imagine **Scene II, 'The Interview'**.
Write an opening dialogue (about 10 lines) between the Personnel Manager and Jason. (10)

Studied drama

The last question in the Drama section asks you about a play or film you have studied. This question is worth **20 marks** and should take you about **ten minutes** to write. That means that you should be able to write at least **three paragraphs** on your play or film.

From your play or film you should know the following:

Key character: Describe the central character in the play or film. How have they changed during the play or film? Describe a key moment in the play or film that changed them.
Key scene: Describe exactly what happens in a key scene in the play or film. Who was involved in the scene? Why was the scene so important? Does it change the outcome of the play or film? How?
Moment of conflict: Describe a scene in the play or film with conflict. Who was involved? Why did the conflict arise? How was it resolved? What happened then? Was there tension? How was this created?

At this stage you should have prepared a play or film to base your answers on for the exam.

- The first line of your answer should state the name of the play you have studied and the author, or in the case of a film, the **name of the film and the writer or director**. So learn to spell the names correctly! For example: 'The play I have studied is *The Field* by John B. Keane.'
- Don't just write about a film you saw recently. You may not know the names of the characters, the director or the place it is set.
- Break your answer into **paragraphs**. These should answer each part of the question separately. For example, a question that asks you to 'describe a scene, explain how the conflict was created and say how it was resolved' should be broken into three separate paragraphs.
- **Practise** writing about the key scenes and characters before the exam.

Sample question

The following extract is from a play called *Our Day Out* by Willy Russell. This extract contains conflict and it reveals something about the characters. Read the extract and see how it is used to answer the question that follows.

In this play, a group of children from Mrs Kay's progress class are brought on a day trip to Conway Castle in Wales. The children are from the backstreets of Liverpool and this trip is a new experience for many of them. One of the children, Carol, doesn't want to return home to her depressing life after the trip. Mr Briggs, a teacher who was reluctant to be on the trip and who doesn't like the children very much, finds her and has to persuade her to come back.

Briggs: Carol Chandler, just come here. Who gave you permission to come on these cliffs?

Carol: *(moving to the edge)* No one.

She turns and dismisses him.

Briggs: I'm talking to you Miss Chandler.

She continues to ignore his presence.

Now just listen here young lady...

Carol: *(suddenly turning)* Don't you come near me!

Briggs: *(taken aback by her vehemence, he stops)* Pardon?

Carol: I don't want you to come near me.

Briggs: Well in that case just get yourself moving and let's get down to the beach.

Carol: You go. I'm not coming.

Briggs: You what?

Carol: Tell Mrs Kay she can go home without me. I'm stoppin' here by the sea.

Pause.

Briggs: Now you just listen to me. I've had just about enough and I'm not putting up with a pile of silliness from the likes of you. Now come on!

He starts towards her but she moves to the very edge of the cliff.

Carol: Try an' get me an' I'll jump over.

Briggs stops in his tracks, astounded and angered.

Briggs: *(shouting)* Listen you stupid girl, get yourself over here this minute.

She ignores him.

I'll not tell you again!

They stare at each other. It's obvious that she will not do as he bids.

I'll give you five seconds! Just five seconds. One, two, three, four, I'm warning you!... Five.

Carol:	I've told y', I'm not comin' with y'. I will jump y'know. I will.
Briggs:	Just what are you tryin' to do to me?
Carol:	I've told y', just leave me alone an' I won't jump. *(Pause)* I wanna stay here where it's nice.
Briggs:	Stay here? How could you stay here? What would you do eh? Where would you live?
Carol:	I'd be alright.
Briggs:	I've told you, stop being silly.
Carol:	*(turning on him)* What are you worried for eh? You don't care do y'? Do y'?
Briggs:	What? About you?... Listen, if I didn't care, why would I be up here now, trying to stop you doing something stupid?
Carol:	Because if I jumped over, you'd get into trouble when you get back to school. That's why Briggsy, so stop goin' on. You hate me.
Briggs:	Don't be ridiculous. Just because I'm a schoolteacher it doesn't mean to say that...
Carol:	Don't lie, you! I know you hate me. I've seen you goin' home in your car, passin' us on the street. An' the way you look at us. You hate all the kids.
Briggs:	What... why do you say that?
Carol:	Why can't I just stay out here an' live in one of them nice white houses, an' do the garden an' that?
Briggs:	Look... Carol... You're talking as though life for you is ending, instead of just beginning. Now why can't... I mean, if that's what you want... why can't... what's to stop you working hard at school from now on, getting a good job and then moving out here when you're old enough? Eh?
Carol:	*(she turns and looks at him with pure contempt)* Don't be so bloody stupid.
	She turns to look out to the sea.
	It's been a great day today. I loved it. I don't wanna leave here an' go home. *(Pause)* If I stayed it wouldn't be any good though, would it? You'd send the coppers to get me, wouldn't y'?
Briggs:	We'd have to. How would you survive out here?
Carol:	I know. *(Pause)* I'm not goin' back though.
	(She kneels at the cliff edge, looks over.)
Briggs:	Carol... please...
Carol:	Sir... you know if you'd been my old feller... I would've been all right wouldn't I?

	Briggs slowly and cautiously creeping forward, holding out his hand.
Briggs:	Carol, please come away from there.
	She looks down over the cliff.
	Please.
Carol:	Sir... sir you don't half look funny y' know.
Briggs:	*(smiling)* Why?
Carol:	Sir, you should smile more often. You look great when y' smile.
Briggs:	*(holding out his hand)* Come on, Carol.
Carol:	Sir... what'll happen to me for doin' this?
Briggs:	Nothin' ... I promise.
Carol:	Sir, you're promisin' now, but what about back at school?
Briggs:	It won't even be mentioned, I promise...
	His hand outstretched. She decides to believe him. She reaches out for his hand. As she does she slips but he manages to lunge forward and clasp her to safety.

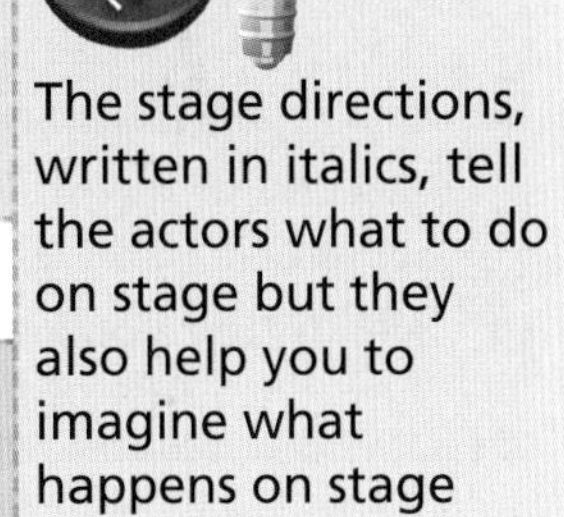

The stage directions, written in italics, tell the actors what to do on stage but they also help you to imagine what happens on stage when you are reading an extract.

Name a play or film you have studied in which something unexpected happens. Describe the unexpected event and explain why it was unexpected. Did the unexpected event add to your enjoyment of the studied play or film?
Why/why not? (20)
(2007, 2009)

Sample answer

The play I have studied is *Our Day Out* by Willy Russell. In this play a group of school children go on a school trip to Conway Castle. The play is set in Liverpool and the children are from the progress class. They have never been away before and cause chaos wherever they go.

One of the children, Carol, didn't want to go home. The unexpected event was when Carol was on the cliff threatening to jump. Mr Briggs, the grumpy, strict teacher told her she was being silly and that she had to go home. Carol said she didn't want to go back there and she moved closer to the edge.

I found this scene unexpected because I didn't expect Carol to react in this way and Mr Briggs was the last person you would want to talk her down from a cliff edge as he was always annoyed by the students.

This scene added to my enjoyment of the play as I didn't know what was going to happen next. Mr Briggs tried to force her to come down by counting to five, but Carol didn't move. This made the scene very exciting. Mr Briggs promised her that he wouldn't say anything to the others and Carol moved towards him. She slipped at the edge and Mr Briggs had to catch her to stop her from falling off the cliff. This created tension in the scene and was very dramatic, which added to my enjoyment of the play.

Answering on a film

When answering this question on a film you have studied, you need to be aware of the same aspects of the film as of the play, e.g. characters, key scenes, moments of conflict, etc.

- Make sure you don't just rewrite the entire plot of the film.
- If you are asked a specific question on a scene or a character, you must limit your answer to that question.
- Make sure you know the name of the director of the film.

Name a play or film you have studied in which a character has an important dream or ambition which he/she succeeds or fails in making real.

- What was the dream or ambition?
- How did it succeed or fail?
- What effect did this success or failure have on the character in question?
- Would you recommend this film or play to your friends? Why/ why not? (20) (2008)

Sample answer on a film

The film I have studied is *Romeo and Juliet* directed by Baz Luhrmann. In this film, the main character, Romeo, has an ambition to marry his love, Juliet. There are many difficulties facing these two characters, as their parents are involved in a feud.

His ambition does succeed, as they marry each other in secret, but they manage to spend only one night together.

The effect the marriage has on Romeo means that he tries to avoid a fight with Tybalt, Juliet's cousin, but ends up killing him. This leads to Romeo's banishment and the misunderstanding that results in the death of both Romeo and Juliet.

I would recommend this film to my friends as, even though the language is Shakespearian, it is very easy to follow. It is set in modern times and the music score and camera shots make it very exciting. Leonardo DiCaprio and Claire Danes are very convincing as the young couple in love and the death scene in the church is very moving. For these reasons I would recommend this film to my friends.

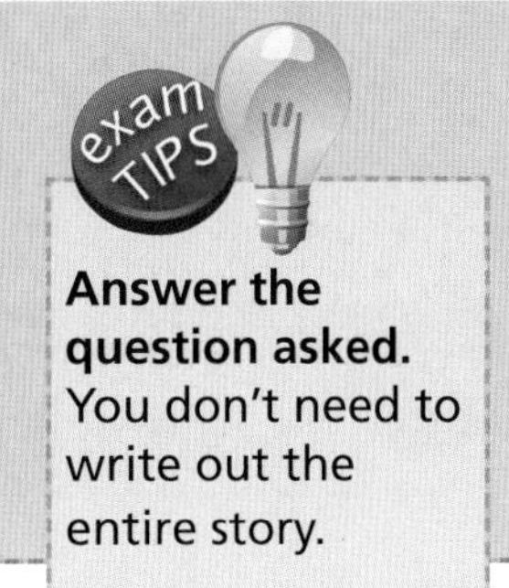

Answer the question asked. You don't need to write out the entire story.

The best way to prepare for this section of the exam is to practise as many questions as you can on the play or film you have studied.

Practice questions

All questions are worth 20 marks.

1. Name a play or a film you have studied.
   Pick the scene you remember best from the play or film and write about:
   - What exactly happened.
   - How any one character behaved.
   - What especially makes you remember the scene you have chosen. (2005)
2. Name a play or film you have studied.
   Using **ONE** of the following headings, write about the play or film:
   - The scene I liked best.
   - The character I found most interesting.
   - Why I found the play/film enjoyable.
   - Why I did not enjoy the play/film. (2004)
3. Think about a play or film you have studied.
   Pick a very dramatic moment from it and write about:
   - What exactly happened.
   - Which characters were involved.
   - How any one character behaved. (2003)
4. Name a play or film you have studied in which a disagreement occurs.
   - What caused the disagreement?
   - Was the disagreement settled? Why/ why not?
   - Were you satisfied with the ending? Give reasons for your answer. (2006)

7 Media Studies

- To understand the key concepts of the Media Studies section.
- To be able to use those concepts in answering exam questions.

The Media Studies section may appear in **Section 4, 5, 6 or 7 of the paper**. If it appears in **Section 4** then it is a **compulsory question.** In this section you are expected to be able to answer questions on different types of media such as advertising, newspapers, information leaflets signs and television.

As with all the other sections on this paper, this section is worth **60 marks** and you should spend approximately **25 minutes** answering the questions. Make sure you look carefully at the marks awarded for each question. A question worth 20 marks should obviously require more work than a 10-mark question.

exam TIPS

As a rough guide, a 10-mark question should have about 10 lines in your answer. A 20-mark question should have up to 20 lines in the answer.

The exam paper will usually be accompanied by an extra colour paper, **Paper X**. This paper has the sample advertisement, leaflet or photographs that you will be asked to examine for this section of the paper. Make sure you correctly identify the section of the paper referred to in the question.

There are a number of key words common to all media that you need to become familiar with when answering a Media Studies question:

For the past number of years, the last question in the Media Studies section has been a **20-mark question**. This question has asked that you complete a task, such as designing a poster or an information leaflet. To gain as many marks as possible, **focus on exactly what the question asks**. If you are asked to persuade an audience, then your answer should try to be persuasive.

Key words for media studies

Purpose

The first thing you need to decide is the **purpose** of the piece. What does it want to do? Advertising wants to **persuade** us to buy the product, a newspaper article wants to **inform** us of an event and an information leaflet wants to **educate** us in a certain area. Once you have identified the purpose, it is easier to see the techniques used to achieve this aim or purpose.

Target market

You should also be able to identify the **target market** for this piece. Who is it **aimed** at? Sometimes the target market is pictured in the visuals, but be careful. An advertisement for hair shampoo may be aimed at the type of people pictured in the visuals, but the target market for nappies isn't babies (as they can't buy them) but parents, as they do the shopping.

Visuals

When you examine the sample of Media Studies included on the exam paper there are two things that you will see:

- The written words.
- Everything else.

'Everything else' is the visual element. This includes the **colours** used in the background, the **people** shown, the **font**, **size** and **shape** of the letters. All of these things are used for a reason. Your job in the exam is to try to identify and explain **why** they are used.

Colours

It is useful to know why certain colours are used. Some colours are **associated with ideas or feelings.** Red, for example, is associated with love and passion but also with danger. Green is associated with nature and freshness, which is why it is often used in advertising for cleaning products. Look at the colours used. Why do you think they are used? What could they be associated with?

People

People in an advertisement or information leaflet can tell you a lot about who it is aimed at. Look at the **clothes** worn**,** the **situation** they are in and especially their **facial expressions.** All of these things will reveal key elements of the advertisement, leaflet, etc. Do the people have **cheerful expressions** on their faces? Is the product associated with their happiness? Do these people represent the target market? Are they used just to grab your attention? Is a celebrity used? If so, see the next point.

Endorsement

Sometimes a celebrity is used in an advertisement to promote it. This is called **celebrity endorsement.** A lot of sports brands use sports stars to promote their products. Sometimes a famous person may allow their name to be associated with a cause they believe in, such as Bono and the 'Make Poverty History' campaign.

Background

Look at the background in the sample given. Remember it was chosen for a reason. Why do you think this background was chosen? Is it very plain, making the key points stand out? Is it very **dark**, giving a grim or bleak appearance? Or is it **bright** and **cheerful**, giving a positive view? Is there any feature that stands out or is unusual? Why do you think it was used?

Letters

Look at the letters used in the writing on the sample – not what they say, but **how they are presented**. Are they **LARGE** and do they dominate the space? Or are they **small** and insignificant? What **colour** is the writing? Look again at the meaning of certain colours. Is red used to grab your attention or is the text simply black and white? Why do you think certain colours are used? Look at the *type of writing* or the font that is used. Does the writer use a very **old** style or a **modern** sleek style? Why do you think this style was chosen?

Logo

A logo is a **symbol** associated with a product or service. Some logos are very recognisable, such as the Nike logo. Others you may not have seen before. A logo is used to sum up the company and represents what they are about. Check if there are any logos in the sample on the paper. What do these logos tell you about the company involved? What colours are used? Do they stand out? Why?

Text

In any advertisement, information leaflet or set of signs or photographs, there will usually be some writing. This is the **text**. You have already looked at **how** it is written, but now you need to look at **what exactly is said**. You need to identify if any of the following two techniques are used:

Slogan

A slogan is a phrase associated with a product or service. The Nike slogan is 'Just do it!' Some are short and catchy and get straight to the point. To make them sound catchy, sometimes rhyme is used: 'A Mars a day helps you work, rest and play' or alliteration (using words that begin with the same letter): 'If you want to have a **c**uppa have a **C**lub'.

Facts

Some advertisements or information leaflets use a lot of factual information to try to persuade you that they are correct. It is up to you to identify the statements that are factual and those that are only opinion. Look out for **language that sounds scientific or the use of statistics**, e.g. '90 per cent of cat owners said their cats preferred it'.

In advertising especially, you may find some of the following features:

- **Buzz words**: Words that are used to make the product sound more attractive. There are usually words associated with certain areas. Skin care uses buzz words like 'age-defying' and cars use words like 'aerodynamic'.
- **Rhetorical questions**: Questions that do not require an answer, such as: 'Are you tired of the same old boring holidays?'
- **Punctuation**: Sometimes punctuation is used to give the written text some excitement, such as using exclamation marks!!!!
- **Special offers:** Some advertisements include special offers or discounts to try to persuade you to buy the product and to grab your attention.
- **Orders:** Some advertisements give you orders telling you to do something: 'Buy this product', 'Just do it!'

In your answers, you should try to include as many of the key words above as possible to explain why the advertisement or leaflet is effective or why you like it.

Also, when you are designing a poster or leaflet, try to include some of the key points listed above.

Advertising

The most common type of question asked in this section of the exam is on advertising. Usually you will be given an example of an advertisement, or sometimes two advertisements on the same topic. You will then be asked to answer questions on these advertisements. You may be asked to:

- Identify the logo or slogan or target market.
- Comment on the visuals or text.
- Compare the two advertisements for similar products.
- Discuss the techniques used.

Look at the advertisements below and on page 93 from the 2008 exam paper and read the questions and sample answers that follow.

To be used in answering SECTION 7 – MEDIA STUDIES

Get out of the bus lane, and into the fast lane

Slogan

Visual

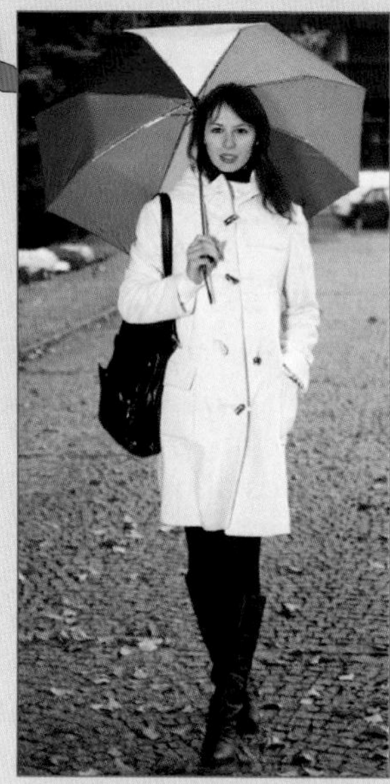

When three full buses in a row rush by you with a gleeful swoosh at 7.30am and you know you're going to be late... when your nice new work clothes are splattered in mud and your neat hair is a wet mess... when you're dying to get to the gig early but the bus doesn't show... when you get stuck sitting beside a smelly person on the bus... when it hits you that you spend over €15.50 a week – €62 a month, €744 a year – to squeeze onto a jam-packed bus and stand the whole way into work... this is when you should seriously start thinking about buying a car of your own.

Negative images

Negative images

If you want independence, if you want a comfy place to listen to your own tunes at your own volume, if you want to get to where you want, when you want, then start looking into insurance, finance and sale deals now.

Positiv image

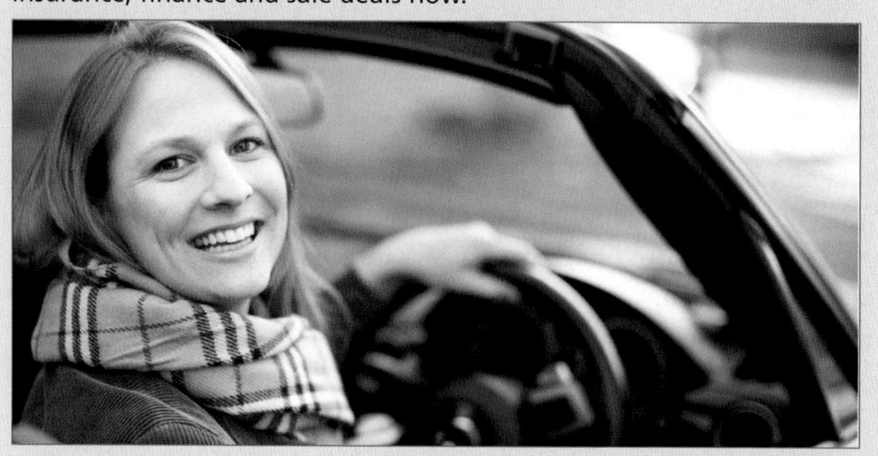

Visu

Get off the bus and into the driver's seat

Sl

Public Transport
It's all the RAGE and none of the HASSLE

Slogan

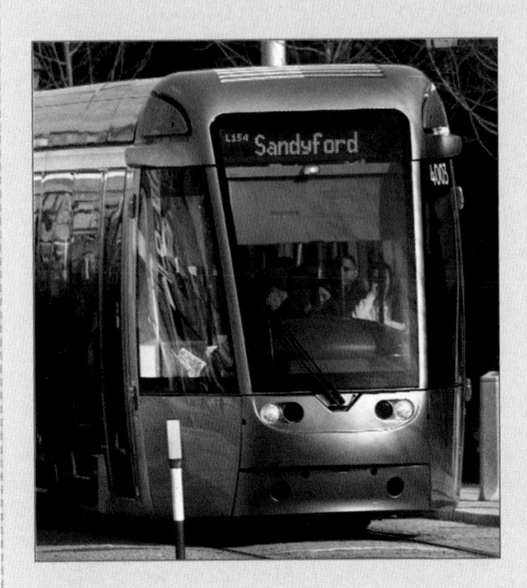

LUAS

The Dublin Luas tram system is a state-of-the-art Light Rail Transit (LRT) System. Luas connects you to Dublin City Centre with a **high** capacity, **high** frequency, **high** speed service. With Luas you will find convenient stop locations, excellent levels of comfort and safety access at all stops.

Repetition

DART

Dublin Area Rapid Transit does exactly what is says – ferries you rapidly from Malahide to Greystones. **Rush hour?** No problem. City traffic jams, parking spaces, stressed out drivers – leave all these behind you. Use our reliable service.

Rhetorical question

A. (i) *According to the text in the advertisement on p. 92, what are the advantages of owning your own car?* *(5)*

According to the advertisement, the advantages of owning your own car are that you can be independent, you have a comfy place to listen to your own tunes at your own volume and you can get to where you want when you want.

(ii) *Are you convinced by this advertisement that it is better to own your own car than to take public transport? Give reasons for your answer.* *(5)*

This advertisement is very persuasive, as it gives a very vivid picture of waiting for a bus. The advertisement describes the frustration of waiting for a bus when you are going to be late, which is very persuasive. It also gives the facts and figures about the cost of using the bus. For these reasons I am convinced by this advertisement.

More than one reason necessary

B. *Which of the advertisements on pp. 92–93 communicates its message more successfully? Give reasons for your answer.* *(10)*

In my opinion, I think the first advertisement communicates its message more successfully. This advertisement uses two very catchy slogans, 'Get out of the bus lane, and into the fast lane' and 'Get off the bus and into the driver's seat'. These slogans give orders to the reader and get the message across to get control rather than waiting on public transport. Also, in the visuals the girl waiting for the bus seems sad and has her umbrella up. The girl in the car seems happy and confident. This communicates the message of the advertisement.

Use quotes from the paper to support the answer

C. *Give examples of exaggeration in the advertisements on pp. 92–93. Give a reason why advertisements make use of exaggeration.* *(10)*

On p. 92 the advertisement uses exaggeration when it says 'three full buses in a row rush by you with a gleeful swoosh', and 'your nice new work clothes are splattered in mud'. On p. 93 the advertisement uses exaggeration when it says 'high capacity, high frequency, high speed service' and 'convenient stop locations, excellent levels of comfort'. I think the advertisements use exaggeration to make their point more clearly. On p. 92, exaggeration makes travelling by bus sound horrendous and on p. 93 exaggeration makes using public transport appear like the logical choice.

D. *Suggest two ways for improving the message in either advertisement. You should refer to:*
- *Texts.*
- *Images.* *(10)*

I think the advertisement on p. 93 could be improved by including images of happy people using their service, as this would link to their slogan, 'It's all the rage and none of the hassle'.

I think the advertisement on p. 92 could be improved by using headings in the text to draw our attention to the key points and by varying the size of the font.

E. *You have been asked to design a poster encouraging people to drive carefully. Describe or draw the poster you would design.*
- *Explain your ideas for the design.*
- *Write a slogan for the poster.* *(20)*

In my poster I would have two photos of a car driving on a busy street. In one photo the driver would be looking to their right and in the next photo the driver would be looking straight ahead but there would be a child suddenly in front of the car. The **facial expression** of the driver and the child would show shock and surprise. The child would wear a red jumper so that the image would stand out. My slogan would be: 'Look closer and slow down'. The **slogan** would be in a large, slanted **font** to grab your attention. The **background** to the advertisement would be black and the slogan would be written in white. The **visuals** and the slogan would focus on how quickly things can happen in busy situations and would encourage people to drive carefully.

See key words used in answer – in **bold**

Information leaflets or brochures

Information leaflets or brochures try to give you information, **educate** you on an issue, or try to persuade you to carry out an action. The **techniques** used in advertising, such as imagery, slogans, etc. are also used in brochures and leaflets to grab your attention.

For example, leaflets on the suffering in the Third World will use an **emotional** photo to grab your attention and the slogan will often use rhetorical questions such as 'Why should they suffer?'

Quite often in the exam, you are asked to design your own advertisement, information leaflet or poster. Your answer should be based on the key elements mentioned above. Divide your answer into the same sections as the question. When writing about how you would present your work, you could divide your answer into the written and visual parts of your design. For example, on the 2004 paper, students were asked to design a healthy living leaflet. The following sample question and answer shows how you could approach the answering of this question.

You are preparing a leaflet on healthy living for distribution in your school.

(i) Write out five points you would include in the leaflet.

(ii) Describe or illustrate how you would present these points on the page.

Sample answers

(i) The five points I would have for my healthy living leaflet would be:

1. Exercise for an hour a day.
2. Eat five portions of fruit or vegetables a day.
3. Drink more water.
4. Cut down on sugary snacks and chocolate.
5. Always eat breakfast.

(ii) I would present these points in the following way:

Written text:

My written text would have to be *eye-catching*, so I would use a large font in red on a white background. My five points would be numbered. I would use a large tick or correct mark to the right of each point to remind people that this is the correct thing to do.

Visuals:

The leaflet needs to make people aware of healthy living, so I would use very *vibrant, bright colours*. I would include a heart *logo,* as this is one of the most important aspects of the leaflet. I would get a celebrity to appear on the leaflet as *celebrity endorsement* catches people's attention. I would use the *slogan* 'Your Health is Your Wealth'. As this *rhymes*, it should be memorable. I would include smaller *photographs* of young people being active, with happy, smiling faces as this is our *target market*. I would use a plain white *background* to make all my main points stand out.

Use the **key words** in your answer.

Examine Paper X below from the 2009 exam paper and attempt the questions that follow.

A

B

C

D

E

F

G

H

What the Campaign is about

In the world today, over 240 million children, some as young as five, are working in full-time employment. Child Labour involves children in the making of bricks, working with machinery in agriculture, carpet weaving, domestic labour, construction work, the making of matches and fireworks, and hundreds of other activities that deny children the right to full-time education.

A. Look at the slogan on visual A of the leaflet on p. 97.
'Stop Child Labour
School is the best place to work'
Do you think this is a good slogan for the campaign?
Give reasons for your answer. (10)

B Examine photographs B–G on the leaflet. Which photograph would you consider to be most effective to use in a campaign against child labour? Give reasons for your answer. (10)

C. Look at the text of visual A and photographs B–G on the leaflet.
Which do you think would give the stronger message for the campaign *'Stop Child Labour school is the best place to work',* the text or the photographs? Give reasons for your answer. (10)

D. Examine photographs D–G on the leaflet. Choose one photograph and state what it tells us about the life of the child, the central figure in the picture. (10)

E. You are asked by your local community newspaper to write an article to encourage people to sign a petition against child labour. You are using photograph H on the leaflet to illustrate the problem.
(i) Write an eye-catching caption for the photograph.
(ii) State two convincing reasons you would use in your article to explain why people should sign this petition. (20)

Make sure you read the question carefully! Part E does not ask you to write the **article**, only to write the **caption** and to state **two reasons** you would use.

Photographs

You may be asked to examine a photograph, or series of photographs, in this section of the exam paper.

- Examine the photographs and make sure you understand exactly **what is being depicted** or shown.
- Look at the questions asked. If you are asked to **describe** a photograph, look back at the hints for describing photographs in the Functionaal Writing section.
- You may be asked to **group** the photographs or to give a **title or written text** for the photographs. See if there are any logical links between the photographs. Do they contain children or animals? Do they show a particular activity? Do they capture a certain time of day? Is there anything interesting about the way the photograph has been captured?
- You may be asked to comment on the **image**, use of **colour** or the **message** conveyed in the photograph.

There are some technical words that may help you to examine the photographs.

- **Foreground**: The area at the front of the photograph.
- **Background:** The area at the back of the photograph.
- **Focus:** The area or item in the photograph that grabs your attention. It's usually found at the centre of the photograph and the image is sharp, not blurred.
- **Low-angle shot:** Where the camera is below the object being photographed and is looking up. This type of shot makes things appear larger than they are and therefore more threatening.
- **High-angle shot:** Where the camera is above the object being photographed and is looking down. This type of shot makes things appear smaller than they are and therefore less threatening.

Practice question

Examine the photographs on p. 100 and answer these questions.

1. For a photography exhibition, you must arrange the photographs into two or three groupings. Give a suitable name to each grouping.
2. Choose one photograph that you feel stands out. Describe the photograph accurately. Explain why you think it stands out.
3. Write a caption and a brief introduction to the photograph that could be included in the exhibition.
4. Which photograph do you feel is the least interesting? Give reasons for your answer.

1

Newspapers

There are **two different types** of newspapers that you need to be aware of:

1. Tabloid.
2. Broadsheet.

You need to be able to identify the key features of each.

Tabloid	Broadsheet
Smaller size	Larger size (usually)
Large headlines, exaggerated	Factual headlines
Large number of photographs	Fewer photographs, more written text
Block headlines	Longer articles
'True life' stories	Politics/world affairs/ business
Celebrity gossip	Analysis of events
Paparazzi photos	Photographs from abroad

The main difference between these two types of newspapers can be seen in the **layout of the front page**. In a tabloid newspaper, the front page is usually dominated by one story with a large photograph, a block headline and very little written text. In a broadsheet newspaper, the front page usually contains a number of stories with smaller photographs and a lot of written text.

EVENING Herald

VOUCHER DAY
MAJOR DISCOUNTS INSIDE SEE PAGES 53-54

FREE DART TICKETS ALL WEEK
SEE PAGE 24

IRELAND'S EVENING NEWSPAPER | WEDNESDAY 18 AUGUST 2010 | €1.20 | CITY FINAL VOL 119 NO 196

YOUR CHANCE TO STAR WITH JEDWARD
SEE PAGE 52 FOR DETAILS

WIN TICKETS TO THE DUBS V CORK PAGE 78

CHILD-KILLER MUM DIES IN PRISON

FEELING A-OKAY AS RESULTS COME OUT

THE WAIT IS OVER: Liz Ferris, Sutton, gets her hands on her Leaving Cert results at Loreto on the Green today SEE PAGES 2-3

DOCHAS DEATH: Inmate suffocates

By Charlie Mallon

A WOMAN who drowned her seven-year-old son has taken her own life in the Dochas women's prison.

Lifer Ruth Murphy (48) murdered her only child by drowning him in the sea off a Co Wicklow beach in 2001.

Today, just over nine years later, she died in jail. Sources said that she suffocated after placing a plastic bag over her head and tying it around her neck.

Murphy, who had her own room, is understood to have gone into a communal area of the prison shortly before she killed herself.

The death of Karl Murphy at the hands of his mother shocked the country. The child was found dead shortly after his father reported him missing.

TURN TO PAGE EIGHT

DROWNED: Karl Murphy (7)

DUBLIN'S NO 1 CRIME GODFATHER ARRESTED P4-5

Evening Herald

Practice question

Look at the examples of newspapers on this page and answer the following questions.

1. What is the main headline?
2. What are the dominant colours used?
3. What do you think is the most eye-catching part of this front page?
4. Would you buy this paper? Why/why not?

irishtimes.com

THE IRISH TIMES

Wednesday, August 18, 2010 €1.80 (incl. VAT) £1.20 Northern Ireland

RESULTS 2010
SPECIAL LEAVING CERT SUPPLEMENT
HELPLINE 1800 946 942

LISTEN TO BRIAN MOONEY'S ADVICE ON A PODCAST AT IRISHTIMES.COM

NewsDigest

€3.2bn bill for Irish Nationwide

Baghdad suicide bombing leaves at least 57 dead

HomeNews

BusinessNews

WorldNews

Donald Clarke: page 14

SportsWednesday

Weather

Index

Veteran of 1929 Pakistan flooding says this is even worse

Failure rates in science and maths confirm system fears

US companies say Leaving Cert subject results 'disappointing'

SEÁN FLYNN
Education Editor

RESULTS MAIN POINTS

50-year-old review reveals the Beatles 'strum too much'

1. How many different stories are featured on this page?
2. What are the dominant colours used?
3. Would you buy this newspaper? Why/why not?
4. What are the main differences between this paper and the previous newspaper?

Magazines

Different magazines are **aimed at different readers**. You can identify who they are aimed at by looking at the types of stories included, the photos used and the products that are advertised. For example, a men's magazine about football is unlikely to contain an advertisement for make-up!

Practice question

Look at the following contents page for a magazine and answer the questions:

heat 27 NOV - 3 DEC 2010

ON THE COVER

6 KATE & WILLS
A beautiful tribute starring Jodie Marsh and Keith Lemon

9 KELLY OSBOURNE
She shows off her smokin' new bod in a bikini

10 CHER VS REBECCA
Rebecca's the favourite. Cher doesn't like it. So she's declared war. There will be tears

14 *HEAT'S* BIG *X FACTOR* SURVEY
Who do you want to win? Who's your favourite judge? We reveal the answers

NEWS & STUFF

22 MICHELLE WILLIAMS
She reveals how dancing and dieting made her look too thin

25 ROCHELLE & MARVIN
She's heartbroken and he's out on the pull. Boo!

35 "DR" GILLIAN McKEITH
The poo-prodding jungle whinger explained

36 KIMBERLEY WALSH
Does the Girls Aloud star want to start a family?

Everybody's talking about...

MIDDLETON'S LOVELY HAIR

Sod the heirloom engagement ring. Forget about the now sold-out blue Issa frock. Who cares about Wills' stammering tales of his proposal? The Royal wedding announcement was all about one thing for us: Kate Middleton's hair. Glossier than any Best In Show at Crufts, with gravity-defying volume and more bounce than a bra-less Christina Hendricks on a trampoline, this is the most jealous we've been of a 'do, *ever*. Either she's taking more than one bottle into the shower or that's the best goddamn weave we've ever seen.

FEATURES

76 *CORRIE'S* 50TH
Blimey, *Coronation Street* is 50! To celebrate, we asked its current stars who they'd most like to see in their birthday suit

78 N-DUBZ
We chat to the cheeky scamps. That Dappy's "single to mingle", apparently

STARSTYLE

88 DANNII VS POSH
They're both fab and they both have fashion labels – but which celebs are wearing what? It's a fashion face-off. Whoop!

111 FEARNE COTTON
She took us shopping to show us her make-up range and give us a few slap tips. Slap as in make-up, not hitting – she's not like that

TV & REVIEWS

117 REVIEWS
JLS' new album is called *Outta This World*. We tell you whether it is

130 *MISFITS'* NAUGHTY BITS
All the ASBO superheroes' rude sayings in one place for you to chuckle at. You're welcome

FOLLOW US!
FACEBOOK.COM/HEATWORLD
TWITTER.COM/HEATWORLD

27 NOV - 3 DEC 2010 WWW.HEATWORLD.COM [[1R]]

1. What types of stories are in this magazine?
2. What colours are used to grab your attention?
3. Who do you think this magazine is aimed at?
4. List four products that you think would be advertised in this magazine.

Television and radio

Before you even look at an exam paper or textbook, you already know quite a lot about these two forms of media. You are exposed to them every day, but before you can answer a question on them you need to be aware of a few key words:

- **National radio station:** This is a radio station that broadcasts to the whole country, e.g.: Radio 1, 2FM and Today FM.
- **Local radio station:** This is a radio station that only broadcasts in a small location. They are mainly concerned with **local** events and provide a service to the local community, e.g.: Clare FM, KFM, FM104.
- **Schedule:** This is a list of shows or programmes and the times they are broadcast. In a television schedule, the station will usually try to cater for the needs of the viewer at certain times. For instance, children's programmes will be shown in the morning and afternoon, and more adult programmes later in the evening.
- **The watershed:** Before this time, **usually 9pm**, programmes must be suitable for family viewing. They should not contain violence or bad language.

Questions on television and radio are quite difficult to include in an exam paper as they are not a printed media. You may be asked to examine a television or radio schedule and to comment on the programmes included. Make sure you keep the key points in mind when attempting the question.

Cartoons

There are **two types** of cartoons found in the media:

1. Political cartoons.
2. Humorous cartoons.

Political cartoons are there to **make fun** of a current political situation or to point out serious issues in a humorous way.

Humorous cartoons are not political but are just **trying to be funny**. These cartoons, such as Denis the Menace or Garfield, are often found at the back of newspapers and may continue on from day to day.

You may be asked questions about the characters in these cartoons and what they are doing. There are some things you need to keep in mind:

1. Refer only to the cartoon on the paper. It doesn't matter if you know that Denis the Menace always annoys his next-door neighbour; if it isn't on the paper, you can't refer to it in your answer.
2. Use all the information on the paper to help you. Look at what the characters **DO** and what they **SAY**. These will be the key points in your answer.

8 Help! Spelling, Grammar and Punctuation

- To understand how to use punctuation.
- To be able to write direct speech and dialogue correctly.
- To identify frequently misspelled words.

Throughout the paper, the examiner will be aware of your **standard of writing**. The examiner will reward you for good use of language and penalise you for bad spelling and punctuation.

In order to write well, you don't need to have long, involved sentences using lots of big words. You **do** need to **make yourself clearly understood**. Keep it simple and avoid some basic mistakes. There are a few common mistakes that can be easily avoided. Keeping an eye out for these points will make all the difference.

Punctuation

Punctuation (full stops, commas, apostrophes, etc.) is there for a reason. It is your way of telling the reader exactly what you mean. Sloppy punctuation means that your work will be very difficult to follow and possibly won't make sense.

Full stop

The most basic element of punctuation is the full stop.

You must have a full stop at the end of every sentence. A question mark and an exclamation mark have the same function as a full stop. Therefore, every sentence you write should end in a full stop, question mark or exclamation mark.

Capital letters

Every new sentence **must** begin with a capital letter. Capital letters are also used for the name of something:

- A person's name, e.g. James Bond.
- The name of a country or place, e.g. Kildare, Ballyhaunis.
- Books or film titles, e.g. *Mission Impossible.*
- Months and days, e.g. January.
- Rivers, mountains, lakes, e.g. Shannon.
- Sports teams, e.g. Manchester United.

Comma

Commas are used to separate items on a list or to divide phrases in a long sentence.

A comma gives the reader an indication where to pause so that the sentence makes sense, e.g. 'I stopped, stared and glanced back again just to be sure'.

Apostrophes

When in doubt, students tend to stick in apostrophes everywhere or else leave them out completely. Either option will leave the examiner trying to guess what you mean, which will result in your losing marks.

There are two occasions when you use an apostrophe:

- To show that a letter is missing, e.g. don't = do not, I'm = I am, you've = you have, they're = they are.
- To show ownership, e.g. Mary's dog, the teacher's apple.

Do **not** put an apostrophe before every 's' – it is incorrect and unnecessary!

If a word is plural (more than one) and has added an 's', (e.g. boys) and you wish to show ownership (e.g. the bags belonging to the boys) then the apostrophe goes after the 's', e.g. the boys' bags.

As with all rules, there is an exception: it is = it's, **but** if you want to show ownership, there is **no** apostrophe, e.g. The horse has lost its shoe.

Direct speech

In your personal writing, you will probably use direct speech at some point, e.g. a conversation between two characters.

Follow these punctuation guidelines to write direct speech correctly.

- Start a new line every time a new character speaks. This makes it easier for the examiner to follow who is speaking and ensures you remember to use quotation marks where necessary.
- The first word in any direct speech is always a capital letter.
- Quotation marks must surround the words that a character says.
- Add a comma before the quotation if it is followed by more writing, e.g. 'Hello,' said Mary.

Look at the following sample to see these guidelines at work.

'Why do we have to go today?' whined Jack, Sarah's little brother.

'Because I said so,' said Sarah, 'and I'm in charge.' She walked ahead of him down the street.

'I'm too tired,' he tried again.

'Hurry up or I'll leave you behind!'

Jack rushed to catch up with his sister, but her long strides soon left him struggling behind her.

Dialogue

When writing dialogue, you don't need to use quotation marks, but you do still need to use other appropriate punctuation. You may be asked to write a dialogue in the **personal writing section** or in the **drama section** of the paper. Look at the following example to see how a dialogue should be written:

Jack: Why do we have to go today?
Sarah: Because I said so and I'm in charge.
Jack: I'm too tired.
Sarah: Hurry up or I'll leave you behind!

Spelling

The following points include some of the spelling rules that seem to cause problems and a list of frequently misspelled words.

Plurals

- To create a plural for most words, simply add an 's', e.g. cars, dogs, doors.
- Some words are irregular and form the plural by changing letters or by staying the same, e.g. children, sheep.
- Words that end in –ch add 'es', e.g. marches, churches.
- Words that end in –o add 'es', e.g. heroes, volcanoes, unless there is a vowel before the 'o', e.g. stereos, videos. Exceptions to this rule include: pianos, solos, halos.
- Words that end in –y change to –ies, e.g. fly => flies, sky => skies, unless there is a vowel before the 'y', e.g. monkeys.
- Words that end in –x add 'es', e.g. box => boxes.
- Words that end in – f or –fe change to –ves, e.g. loaf => loaves. Exceptions to this rule include: chiefs, cliffs, roofs.

Other spelling rules

- 'i' before 'e' except after 'c', e.g. thief, receive. Exceptions to this rule include: eight, either, weird, neighbour, sleigh.
- **There/their/they're:** Learn when to use each of these words, as this is the most common mistake Junior Certificate students make:
  – There = a place or a statement, e.g. 'It's over there', 'There are too many people here.'
  – Their = belonging to them, e.g. their bags, their coats, their hats.
  – They're = they are, e.g. 'They're very tired.'

Frequently misspelled words

Check the following list for words that you frequently misspell and learn how to spell them correctly.

accept
awkward
beginning
character
choice
choose
chose
conscience
conscious
definitely
disappointment
dissatisfied
except
guard
naive
panicked
prejudice
principal
principle
probably
psycho
quiet
quite
rough
said
sincerely
skilful
thought
through
tough
vicious
violent

Acknowledgments

For permission to reproduce copyright material the publishers gratefully acknowledge the following:

'Tidy Towns' by Kieran Fagan reprinted by permission of the author and *The Irish Times*. *Pirates – Fact or Fiction* by Stewart Ross reprinted by permission of Aladdin Books. *The Wonders of the Modern World* by Ann Halliday. *Pirates!* by Celia Rees published in 2009 by Bloomsbury Publishing PLC. *The Wish List* by Eoin Colfer first published by The O'Brien Press ltd, 2000. 'Online Shopping' by Chris Johns from *The Irish Times*, 3 May 2006. 'Misson Impossible III' by Michael Dwyer from *The Irish Times*, 5 May 2006, reprinted by permission of *The Irish Times*. Extract from *H.I.V.E* by Mark Walden reprinted by permission of Bloomsbury Publishing. 'The Sniper' from *Spring Sowing* by Liam O'Flaherty (Copyright ©The Estate of Liam O'Flaherty 1924) is reproduced by permission of PFD on behalf of the Estate of Liam O'Flaherty. The extract from *The Door* by Margrit Cruickshank, first published in 1996, is reprinted by kind permission of the author through the Jonathan Williams Literary Agency. 'One Question From a Bullet' by John Agard reprinted by permission of The Caroline Sheldon Literary Agency Ltd. 'My Gramp' Copyright ©John Foster 1991 from *Four O'Clock Friday* (Oxford University Press) included by permission of the author. 'Pachy the Dinosaur' from *A Dozen Dinosaurs,* text copyright © Richard Armour 1967. Published in Great Britain in 1975 and used with permission of Egmont UK Ltd London. 'Mid-term Break' by Seamus Heaney and 'The Early Purges' by Seamus Heaney as well as 'Tich Miller' by Wendy Cope reprinted by permission of Faber and Faber Ltd. 'The General' and 'Base Details' by Siegfried Sassoon copyright Siegfried Sassoon by kind permission of the Estate of George Sassoon. 'The Listeners' by Walter de la Mare reprinted by permission of the Literary Trustees of Walter de la Mare and The Society of Authors as their representative. 'Fight!' by Barrie Wade. 'In my life' lyrics by John Lennon/Paul McCartney. Copyright 1965 Sony/ATV Music Publishing LLC. All rights administered by Sony/ATV Music Publishing LLC. All rights reserved. Used by permission. 'Lovers (Winners and Lovers)' by Brian Friel reprinted by kind permission of the author and The Gallery Press, Loughcrew, Oldcastle, County Meath, Ireland from *Lovers* (1984). Play 'Just the Job' by Ann Farquhar-Smith reprinted by kind permission of the author. *Our Day Out* by Willy Russell reprinted by permission of Pearson. Copyright © 1984, 1991 by Willy Russell. All rights whatsoever in this play are strictly reserved and application for performance etc., must be made before rehearsal to Casarotto Ramsay & Associates Ltd., 7–12 Noel Street, London W1F 8GQ. No performance may be given unless a licence has been obtained.

The publishers have made every effort to trace copyright holders, but if they have inadvertently overlooked any they will be pleased to make the necessary arrangements at the first opportunity.